THE COLLECTED BOOKS OF ARTIE GOLD

compiled and edited by

Ken Norris & Endre Farkas

TALONBOOKS

Talonbooks
P.O. Box 2076, Vancouver, British Columbia, Canada V6B 3S3
www.talonbooks.com

Typeset in Adobe Garamond and printed and bound in Canada.
Printed on 100% post-consumer recycled paper.

First Printing: 2010

The publisher gratefully acknowledges the financial support of the Canada Council for the
Arts; the Government of Canada through the Book Publishing Industry Development Program;
and the Province of British Columbia through the British Columbia Arts Council and the Book
Publishing Tax Credit for our publishing activities.

The editors would like to thank Odette Dube for her help with this book.

LIBRARY AND ARCHIVES CANADA CATALOGUING IN PUBLICATION

Gold, Artie, 1947–2007
        The collected books of Artie Gold / compiled and edited by Ken
Norris and Endre Farkas.

Poems.
ISBN 978-0-88922-652-4

        I. Norris, Ken, 1951– II. Farkas, Endre, 1948– III. Title.

PS8563.O827A17 2010   C811'.54   C2010-902234-3

CONTENTS

Artie Gold as Light Fixture

Jack Spicer always said that he didn't care if his poems weren't being read in New York or Duluth; he had an audience in the Bay Area for the 250 copies someone might print. In the middle of 1965 he died at age 39, and that was that for a while. When I arrived as a writer in residence in Montreal in 1967 I didn't expect to find anyone who had read Jack Spicer. But nothing could have prepared me for the young man who went by the signature "A. Gold." Not only had he read Spicer, but he wanted to *be* Spicer, as long as he could also be Frank O'Hara, another poet not habitually read by the literary and academic folks on that Island in the St. Lawrence River.

It was not until 1975 that the San Francisco poet was published to a wider geography, in that year's *Collected Books of Jack Spicer*. Spicer's practice was not to write occasional poems or loose lyrics, but to be working on a book, and he had a lot of personal procedural rules about what that entailed. Sometimes Artie worked on a book. But if you saw his kitchen or his shoulder bag you would see great heaps of paper upon which A. Gold poems were handwritten or typed. People would see him coming and duck back into the alley, unwilling to spend their whole weekend reading these newest pages.

Still, I think that it is a good idea to gather the books of Artie Gold into one volume. And there are rumours that some of the other hundreds of poems that have not totally disappeared will constitute another volume some time somewhere, just as a collected Spicer has now been published.

I make the Spicer connection partly because of Artie's avowed interest, of course, and partly because I know how the official literature custodians can and do ignore the most interesting poetry being written in their country. Since 1967 I have seen a lot of good young poets arrive, and I have been so damned glad that they can still find their way somehow to my ears. When Artie died at age 60 who could believe he was ever that age? He passed on Valentine's Day 2007, the most garrulous poet who ever had to hide away from people because of his allergies. And the obits writer from a Montreal daily asked me whether he should spend space on this "poet," or was he "just another of those Montrealers revered for their admirably careless lifestyles?"

Artie used to send you surprises in the mail, strange objects, drawings he made of you years ago, little geodes, words that had to be dangled in the window's light before you could make them out. His poems could be like that, too. He had an acutely sensitive ear and a willingness to make sounds you would never expect. His images leaped from porch rail to nose cone, and he wove smart-alec irony through sharp threads of emotion. You knew that he was watching, and that his amused eyes were on you when you lifted your face from the page.

Life handed Artie a lot of miserable obstacles from the beginning, some old family sadness you would never hear all of, bad lungs that could not abide the cats he liked so much, hunger for company he had to avoid more and more. Maybe he really was a *poète maudit*, as he is often limned; but I don't remember elsewhere seeing such a combination of gift and application in a young practitioner. And just now I caught a glimpse of the look on his face that told me how funny he thinks that sentence is.

In my introduction to *cityflowers* you will find my delight in the sheer capability of this Montreal poet in his twenties, so much unlike the others with their academic structures and desire to express themselves. All these years later I still don't know how that young man found the means to educate himself so well. As I have said, his only contemporary in 1969 Montreal was Dwight Gardiner, who also loved Spicer and O'Hara. By 1974, Gardiner was in Vancouver, working at Talonbooks, where he designed *Even yr photograph looks afraid of me*.

I was living in Vancouver too, and for a while Artie came out to live here, where he would teach west coast poets to guard their refrigerators and practice their irony. Artie had previously spent time in California, but the Pacific was really no place for A. Gold — he needed to be within reach of the chicken liver at Snowden Deli.

Little Gold books came out just about every year in the seventies, and in their unique bindings and designs they illustrated Artie's penchant for curios. *Mixed Doubles*, co-authored with Geoff Young and hand-printed at The Figures in San Francisco, looks like a tennis court, complete with net. *5 Jockeypoems* comes as a fold-out inside an envelope, produced by a sympatico Montreal bookstore, The Word. *Some of the cat poems* is a handy chapbook that also features Artie's witty and precise cat drawings, as well as a preface by "The shortstop of the heart." Though I was a shortstop at the time, the preface is not by me this time, but by Artie himself, his cat-self. *before Romantic Words* came out at the end of the decade, and in my copy Artie wrote "many years in the preparation," a description that, if you read through the poems, seems patently untrue, unless by this time Artie was Jack Spicer and Frank O'Hara.

My introduction to Artie's selected *The Beautiful Chemical Waltz* contains remarks about poems that were in the books mentioned above. It could almost serve as an introduction to the present collection, and I stand by everything I wrote there. I did not see my young friend very often in the last years of his life — once when he was dumpster-diving for antiques in some happening part of downtown Montreal, finally at the door of his apartment on west Sherbrooke. I went to Montreal to attend his memorial at The Word bookstore on April 14, 2007, where I was pleased to find that the place was jammed and the chicken livers were delicious. All the people Artie had to stay away from were crowded in, an allergic's nightmare. I met Artie's brother for the first time. The poets he had worked with at Véhicule were there, all grown adults. I felt like a ghost, and thought about wafting through Artie's world. I found myself inside my favourite A. Gold poem, "R. W. II." I used to tell young poets to stay away from similies, and now I was brought to my knees by the figure that ends that poem.

— *George Bowering*

CITYFLOWERS

*for Mary Brown
and G.B.*

When I moved to Montreal in 1967 it was with a head full of reveries about the great days of English-language poetry in the city, the forties feuds and the fifties, that delta fanning out full of little mags and coffee shops. In the sixties it was all gone, the avant-garde gone to Vancouver and Toronto. New Wave Canada never splashed as far East as Kingston. The hotshot young poets of 1960 Montreal were dead, quiet, or gone — Leonard Angel, Henry Moscovitch, Stevie Smith, gone.

I found a lot of poets but no community of poets. Delta was still publishing young writers, but they were not of the world, that Mexcity-SF-Vancouver-Toronto-Detroit-NY complex. Montreal was having an after-dinner drink. The young ones weren't poets — they were out on the highway, learning to play a guitar. Montreal is a city of fashion. In 1967 it was no longer the fashion to hang around a bookstore, much less to run one.

So in the years 1967–1971 I encountered lots of young Montrealers who wanted to be poets, but only two who wanted to step fully into the world, the world of poetry. These were Dwight Gardiner and Artie Gold. The only two I knew with holes in the knees of their jeans and great big libraries at home. Of course they were not in a hurry to get published, and of course they got to know each other. They both became familiar with the energy centres of Canadian and American poetry. Curiously they were the first 21-year-olds I ever saw getting turned over by the great dead poet of SF, Jack Spicer, and the great dead poet of NY, Frank O'Hara.

So in this sober collection you will encounter unusual erudition, unusual sophistication for a first book. You'll wonder where the Hell the images came from, because they won't be your regular lyric interpretations of the street scene — that was the way of a decade earlier, well taken care of by Seymour Mayne and Co. Artie's experience, he says, will:

> make me shiver as if
> I were tied on my back
> for many hours
> to a glacier
> that was a sawmill
> in its deadliness.

I feel as if all the shit work we did with *Tish* and *Open Letter* was worth it when I hear Artie Gold's music. He and Dwight can walk in and out as often as they like thru the doors we had to teach ourselves to hang. And they can do what Frank O'Hara did in an emergency: "Turning, I spit in the lock and the knob turns."

That is to say, especially don't come to these poems expecting to find a *reference* to the world, or a reference to Artie Gold's world of feeling and perceptions. Be prepared to step into a world. The poem is, as Jack Spicer said to Lorca, "a collage of the real."

— *GB   Van   11/7/74*

novel

A very large ball of twine. all the highways I've made mistakes along
examine a length like a swimmer's arm. drawn up to th shoulder. 23 miles
Boulder to Golden freezing sleet rockies foothills past th flatirons.
friend i'd dropt out with frm guadalajara passt joint back forth shivered.
don't remember his name. hip though. Valley hiway 115 arvida to aurora
another friend, ford. blue small but very powerful. no cops saw us.
 but leaving colfax one left turn their flashing red plastic drencht us.
have you ever seen th st louis arch gleaming in the neon fresh of crisp
diamond morning? have you ever ferried down west 6 usa gotten off 80cents
past larimer walked th small wide streets of predawn quaint beer-town?
ever seen moose mother with 1 brat rush th tarmac of foggy outer marathon
ever kiss a midnight laundromat table hello after coasting durango gorges?
found green river pleistocene mammals teeth turned opal eyesockets onyx?
shot novocaine understood fire engines. fine-rolled steel arguing morality.
it is late but it is early. It is so cold i feel illegal i enter the icy
darkness push off with one arm glide past only fish.afterwards my silver
ring begins to leave my finger for the clay-dark bottom. i never followed
never touched it again never went where it went. i was totally responsible.
my body projecting above the glass offered itself to mosquito rapids
like the eye crossing white water. not like mercury in a watchglass no.

*

Only pretending to be lawnmower & garden snippers
my jaw's stringy muscles warbled in
birdswing beating membranes into air
for the resonance of orange sound hum,

God only knows what you were being
dropped over me like a kidnapper's hood
yet slower I thought smiling surely I'll
be driven inside out

wandering over flapping apple green
spume coxcomb to gentle pastures
so far from travelled ocean routes that
yes I was walking ridge sun glint
running down slow   a moving ring
lullabies in all the artificial flavors.

*

the beautiful chemical waltz

I'm always absolutely

sure that as I walk
into the kitchen spoon palmed
                very amateurishly

    she will say to me
in a way that will, yes,
        break my heart,
      not to ask her   also
to bow before
                the mechanics of junk

                    when daily
she stirs her coffee to sweet
with what she
must regard   the purged ,
                    very
        decanter of
            all   ails   &
                evils
    that travel my condition.

*

Having nothing to do apart, the two
pick petty quarrels and argue in a low voice ,
his manner — one of that patience that is necessary to be there,
in infinite amount and abundance . for him
it is a kinder act than tolerance or merely
understanding much about her . little
about his own bent body .
somewhere on some stored limb is a wedding vow —
somewhere is a long complaint that became irregular,
once brought the two closer together .
especially visible is the movement of his hand,
raised , lowered , back to his side ,
beating the argument
cryptically , at her foolish sense .
at her uncommon sense
at her foolish sense.
they are at my home as they go through
their lives , quickly , the part that exists
between their marriage and their deaths
, and are dumb to my presence.

*

Alice B Toklas. Alice b to klasal issbe
to klasalass beetoe klassbee klass
beeklassal isbeetoe klassbee
tokalbee lissklass beclassto
beekal towissk lassis beetoe
beekal issliss toebee be be
beto to tobee toe toe
toe toebee be be be klasstoe
klassbee klass eeklass ee
klassee eeass assee kuhlass
lass beekal kalbee ass lass
kliceklass tbee toe teetoe ote
totetet ote et etowet-etowet tab
lablasslab bal bas ball
lob-ball kobble becass lassbee
-un un un ,lassbee un ,un,
bekasslass beeun un un un
bekass
lesbian an an an an
        - na na na
    - siss siss siss
kiss kiss   klit
klitless quick clitcliss
kitless quick clitkiss
oquick kiss okiss
alice suz suz suz
alicuz a a biss
ocome quick kissalissusabiss   o-
kissalissusabissandcomequick
ocomequicklass comequick
beequickinkissingalissus bigclit
kissalissusbigclit sowalissil talkless
ocomebeequickandkissoldalissbee
talklessandcomeandkiss
alice B Toklas.

*

17

Please stay
            and I leaned into her eye
saw only dark prerogatives
                        and flinched,   once
     twice,   three times

(I leaned into her eye
                gathering invectives
          saw old men eating baloney
     and began to panic

only half of what I did was an act)

she said
please stay   and I
threw my arms around her
twisting my head another way

          old men eating picnic
                        baloney sandwiches
huddled across old picnic grounds
that were deserted
          (the wind threw about
          wax sandwich bags
                        and the grass
had mustard stains
                on its tips.
please stay she said
this time
          a second had passed
and I looked back at her
   and without cursing her
(or altering my voice from its usual manner
                              I said: well

     I guess things
   might just
work out.

                    *

18

Sometimes I wish I could see myself —
gaining the door, arteries pounding deaf to all outside noise;
a neural cartoon possessed within my hulky body,
the neon-pipe-cleaner man flashing panic, red
floods my extended reaching hand-flat pink package,
then those sausage-fingers with a desperacy
akin to zen, scrabble at the lock, then
scrabble at the knob ; the door, my chest,
Everything/
Implodes!
(as inwards I lunge; I rush ; sweep the floorboards
up to my chest holding them dear/ in a love-waltz.

Sometimes others do see me
negotiating sanctum in such flurry
& wonder what to make of me

I, each, necessary retreat, never fail
To put the fear of back-bone screeching alley-cat
So deep-planted into every twitching muscle
& nerve, each nerve of all three of my housecats .
They move about unsteadily, jerkily hours later
Suddenly displaced inches beside where they were
as violently , directly,
as if I'd indeed slapt them with a swung gazette.

and I laugh
and I poke fingers to dimples of both cheeks
and I switch my head in relief
to demonstrate to full extent
just how bad it might have been
if I'd been a second later, latching my door .
and I sweat, roll my ears and mop
my warm brow dry for more sweat to gather at
wishing to empty my self of adrenalin
relax for a week, for a day for a lifetime, for a
minute even , safe inside
Fort Poetry . where I do drink from its preserving grace.

*

I want to make the space around the poem
real . solid as the air about kilos of cotton
or the air things fall between
my muse must be a neighbor with
a street address . others may see enough
silhouette sexily bending by a drawn curtain
it is late for them though , I may visit her
whenever I am able / she waits for me only
my muse invisible except when her giving
to me is apparent for others to see .
There can be no jealousy with a
poem so well defined . Not a
shaky idea I have picked up / not
a coincidence that I dwell there ,
· nor a thing easily undone . so real in fact .
a rent is paid.

*

don quixote & son

Foreheads alone
twisting like heartbeats
we want to be one and the same they say
parts of myself
parts of my father
stand on tiptoes pushing so earnestly
out of our two brows
they might touch

but they cannot come together
strong desire & strong desire

my father
myself
clean his oblong swimming pool
  with metal arms from other worlds.

*

In Montreal
covers pulled
          over
my father wears
pajamas ,
pajamas wear
          my father

under the candel
labra and a
low ceiling of
organ notes
my father's
stillness shouts

organ notes back
ground music to
a 40's melodrama
clear just
the chapel ceiling
                    but
the chandeliers
do not tinkle as
the air queers

the organ notes
riding hard into
the canyon
      that
my father
      lies
          boxed
      so well are you
      faking

          get up
          get up
                    I begin

I used to think of him
            his hate, outdistancing
     his understanding . . .
                              now —
     twice, my hand jumps at the bone
his death is a great shock that
     I cannot express
I wonder why he died like that?
     now, his living seems
so perfect!

     get up
and do it/
          again.

                    *

An elm leaf scoops baskets of air
emptying them out on either side and drifts down
and dies.
Maple leaf detaches itself telegraphed at its shadow.

When wind concentrates for several seconds
elm boughs begin to strangle; shaking-off
dancehalls of jitterbugging green scars;

these like the fiddles of benzedrine-gypsies
arc and bow in too small a space
like a badly catered shriner's affair;

brother maple holds his peace stubbornly
though Autumn must embarrass him.
Not escaping a newly-dead-dog , will his fleas pour out;
rather he would quietly empty the room.

*

the illegal swimmer

Not realizing the night,
accepting the cold the water's arrogance

breaking into the water; intruding
in an element with no love
so men are fooled and drowned.

mercury it will slide,
rush up our bodies;
and we are returned to earth.

my foot feels the water
slide never embracing it
steps aside.

we might sooner cherish silver.

*

When it becomes cold
and cold flies thru my window like a white bird
or an ice necklace the seasons

tired of fire in August
spilt on my chest;
difficultly

I rise like smoke
on any winter day
in

photo bursts, or series
each so clean
distinct from the other

caught up by its strong pulse
sympathetically
as tho

there were no mistakes
never another Spring
would it suffer
if it had its way —

*

my home is not coloured any colour;
　　　nor is it comfortable; not so much as
uncomfortable/　my reasoning relief waiting here for me
precludes
　　　any such luxury.
there are no seconds, no choices
no places
I'd rather be.　places
I'd rather not be
having filled the house.

　　　　my home is only a condition
　　　　that streets and other buildings
　　　　fail me in.

　　　I produce this dream to satisfy the outside,
little more than the area that I can clear
buoying each elbow out from my hips;
carefully not defending a single drop of air
not absolutely already to be inhaled/ not one they
outside could ever imagine
within their reach.

so the carpets　the chairs　the floors
I stride across — they mean nothing to me, little more)
trees I hide behind while rushing a quick retreat.

　　already I see
　　　　　my shadow battling steps
　　　　　　　　　folding
to my feet.

*

The unit of human noise is a bazaar
likewise matches are blown from a windowsill
the complication bred mistakes even before
it became this complicated little errors like love
returned to and is hollow and empty   yet there is still
the noise   the damned noise from the street   the streets

an avenue that is an ocean   but in the middle
of land   why say dry land   there is no coast
there are no beaches   no places to get off
no reflection or
edge shadows may bend about   at right angles
sure, though, there are bits of mirrors
you might see two objects reflected   your face
someone else's smile but it is spread out there are no corners
for calendars   only a dizzying shimmer here.

so there are no days and day-ends, no
horizons that are constant   and my head slips
with the weather and the sentiment of the noise. and there are ghosts

there is not that tide that meets change or resistance
no glass balls from Japanese fishing fleets to hit rocks
or beachcombers   no shore activities, congress
of old faces   old places   here in the middle
these hang on like the rain. The ocean is too large to ever become
a polluted, overfamiliar scene   unless rocks are exposed
here and there and hang on to cultures for a few thousand years
and therein lies our difficulties. You and I have drunk from
the same coke bottle the same important echo source
so many times been battered about cruelly and recognized it
wanted to get off for something new or throw old things
over a shoulder but the commerce is done to us. we are old nouns,
nouns that follow sentence order, acted upon, nursed.
There is no pride to be had in that constant act.

She brings me water and acts familiar
is a comfort to the photographer and I
am fully bored and mounted from afar as postcards;
reputation and wealth are the negative

there will be relief from the posing of our heads
when we are spread thin like only the most familiar mountains
and then may die going about business as ordained by life.

Is my life indeed that which is slowing progress
are old ideas saluted and posed for like whores that have become
over the years free the act so familiar
the tides outlast the moon ?

*

In the morning her eyes
      are dry, creased with grey
at their edges; the skin
                has stretched
ceased
       to lend any smile to her face.

              dead things,
      moving backwards
into the head.

       I saw you
through a hole
      in the sky
           in front of me
extending outward from my eyes
              I saw
     a blackbird
hop through your eyes
        into your head. I saw you look for it
over your shoulder.

     *

Unlike you
            a photograph of you,
                        lasting,
a Spanish summer
                beside a clock
because you were so much more
perfect
in my memory.

beside you   a cathedral
                        of Gaudi, a beautiful
impermanent cathedral achieved
thru the action of his death
on th people of Barcelona, but you

shoving squids into your Canadian mouth
making the action seem
totally obscene (I was jealous seeing
how much th camera
had totally ignored me

while th cathedral breathed, melted
as much as a barberpole.

            I am standing beside you
in th background, my knee bent,
a foot propped up against a ledge of plaster
(th sun is smiling,   informally
and th shadows edge toward
first storey windows of some buildings).

and you smiling shamelessly
as if you knew you would remain
longer than either of us deserved to
                        didn't give a damn
to think why this would be

knowing the bearer of an image in a crowd
would always be the only real target
of any age.

                        *

The sea lustrous as a snake's belly
th thousand scales delicately
burning   incandescent   flotsam
of overhead sun   baseball   diamonds
                              by the million
hinged as seen   overhead from airplanes
approximate scales   little diamonds
approx
          imate

          (and they are milky in texture as they rock
to and fro   as th sea does

          one great quilt beginning in Boston Harbour and
extending to Lisbon
like a net for falling acrobats
                              and
                    Icarus's
who lifted by the fact the sun is warm follow it
                              its beams, the area
          shone down on

                    capturing azures and coppers
          hopelessly on fractional
                    canvasses.
                              The sea is not
                    exotic
                              the sea
                    is mediterranean
                         middle
               of the earth   the sea
                    is birth
                    the sea is the floating gestures
branches on it make, rocking
                              to and fro
               with green berries
               and wood splinters
                              of men who
     desire passage   at certain speeds.

the sea is   interrupted life of liquid gold

                             (th dark blues and azures
  are man's
anticipation.

*

'You know life passes us by so unnoticed'
until one day we begin to paint it on our eyes.

I stuck a paint brush in my eye and it
sparkled like Jack Frost;
colouring book heroes
appeared on my block
climbing out of windows
grasping the sills
with wet handprints

and it was cold and the moon
was a blue blur.

I yelled that there were other histories
distinct possibilities that had not occurred to me before
and asked who it was that I had addressed

and it was cold and the moon
was a blue blur
                    (and the air
was silent as a leaf.

                    It was funny (your
calling me names
                    this early
in the morning) at a time when the sun
was neither very warm nor yellow;
                    when the air
was silent as a leaf.

'you know life passes us by so unnoticed'
until one day we learn how to sing.

                            *

Remember which way the sun comes up   &   east
or west   it rises anyway
but for the sun
our friendship
does not exist

You are a prayer rug,
                    Turkish,
I am a silver Moorish coin
with the Pillars of Hercules
I am in your pocket
you are down on your knees
worshipping the sun
wherever it sets

the cloth is worn where your knees left and right
have sunk and risen every day
I cannot tell you which has worn more
or how you've pointed the rug
not knowing
which way the sun will set.
perhaps your knees have worn too

perhaps you'll take me out
and spend me on a pastry
after you have prayed.

which hand will touch me
where will the sun be
which knee will touch me ?

*

will rogers poem

A country can have a history,
It is enriched by a population.

breaking its borders, reshaping
its position;   its attitude
from whatever side viewed
                              outside/inside
from whatever people
                    inside/outside

        a rope follows it as it does
                        what it does
much like a lariat being twirled
                            always modified
            within/without
by the hand of the cowboy twirling
/it drives towards
where it isn't just then
wobbling to&fro
or perhaps
is short-lived (the cowboy
inexperienced, or,
overambitious, the knot holding the circle
retraces the bond
slipping into thin air,
and spilling the illusion.

*

The orange tomatoes (these
you couldn't in any honesty call red
if you'd seen them fat falling-ripe
bending the vine, the 50 kilometers of coast
down to the sea as they did
                              salting themselves
where the sea came in
— the sand is white and the water blue or green
        and the sugar cane
growing like malacca
that was too sweet a bottle
local cream soda the kids'd sell you
when you left the coast
began the climb over the Sierras
                Granada, Granada,
I could just say that name
                over and over

                        *

Drifting further than casual sleep
their grandmother stiffened in her chair
to be discovered in the morning
her flesh grey-white, draping bones
like masts of deserted rafts
involved with sailcloth, while channel 12
commercials advised her dead sensibilities
to buy name brands, which had she wakened
she would have bade her daughter do.

Sand covered the floor about the hard wooden chair
but her spirit didn't rise up from her body, it sat
too tired; and she was removed in the morning

by a slow
ambulance
that might have walked to its garage
holding her hand
had she been able. There were no vague circumstances
about the stiff they'd kept in the little room
overnight, knowing her rocking chair
was no longer active.

She was removed without pretense
before her bones might creak
and clatter onto the hardwood
frightening the children
in the next room. The morticians
would be damned if they couldn't get
her tired old face
in customary smile.

*

Who said
jews could never look
into the sun ? I crave

that heat that dazzling
every hour
for my white skin
cannot live in caves, this
for white
salamanders
with white veins, in pools
light never reaches.

The moon's poetry
does so little to me
I do not find a subtlety
in silver allegro. It is
the golden notes we are
denied   make me shiver as if
I were tied on my back
for many hours
                    to a glacier
that was a sawmill
in its deadliness.
Oh Jesus

          to race about the world
evading seasons/to give up
my junkie form/to live
more subtly
as isomorph.
Oh Jesus
how hot the sun has gotten
even in an hour!   Perhaps
what I really wanted was not the sun
but some metaphor
for yellow
imbued on a white moon.

*

This is not a list. it must therefore be a foot; a hand; a movement : a
moving hand or foot or/. Defeat is an arrow riding away from this as
words develop. a new territory is created for the eye. it is always
pleasing to see movement, when it is noticed. I am telling you now of
many things I would tell you of of which these are of those. At the drop
of a handkerchief; a stubborn habit: new things develop. because there
was their need/they have footsteps which trace the state of mind to
us and then we are ourselves. Perhaps a movement and we advance ahead
and this is that is exciting. Our lives, our excitements, less so, our
pleasures, they are recreations of footsteps where there needs be walking
moving, hands, feet, these disturbances of the space about us: where if
we move, someone else, not even else, sits bored or not moving either,
where we might have been. When we stay there, do not think that there
cease to be footsteps for they do not fall but are, waiting, during
our lives as we do or don't. If we see these footsteps and they exist
unmade, then we see the places where we might but are not proceeding;
this makes us hollow; this makes us unsung. the song, there, cannot ever
be unsung, the song, unlike footsteps is too definite, and shows in itself
change of attitude and weight and can carry. we cannot see the song
like footsteps without the rhythm of the man, the foot, the hand that
moved to make the footsteps real.

*

Green grass & melons
vines trailing
and the fingernails of O'hara
something washed ashore in the night ·
day gazed on.
a gulliver unlikely to interest smaller folk
dragonfly grasshopper cricket itinerant bee
all would walk him like tourists who peer
from small hills at objects pamphlets advertise-
before too long engaged in some other activity.

these tiny creatures laid him a cockrobin shroud
a million miles from home & Central Park
a million miles from most real places

where sand grew in patches as the field

scurried off after the ocean like a dog on a scent
stretching the occurrence of green sand plants
thin as sandpiper's feet (& scarce again as sandpipers).

also, toes curled dreamily like brambles
far short of the lapping salt fusillade
the sea at night fires out towards the darkened knee of land.

nothing stood between O'hara & the sea
but a handful of impossible footprints

across a shoulder of the shrinking world of land,
land which lay like O'hara, flung out amongst
      a traffic of stems & flower stalks standing
                              like a crowd
catapulting this deceptively casual unwound man
along with stars and wildflowers & bits of broken planet
to stillness past the inclination to be acted upon,
                              or, unto
rolling like dice onto a picnic spread ,
the dice faces each, blind as Homer .

*

outside my bus endless dirt shoulder passes in the prayer of endless beads counted
different lifetimes seen as billboards flat 2 dimensional black & white distances
I go 61 hrs one time in the nights of dusty south Miami through Texas to Denver
A stop is hot gravy trays tasting hot dogfood meatloaf mashpotatoes always
cast, slowly tick unwind whipping the length of lives sideways & parallel strung
burnt matches faces suffocate against metal bars with upholstered chrome rug
no book smoothly read these light hours dreams of me inside cave of leg
being born & warm not surfacing being carried fluids embalming foetuses.
the air is Miami air until Savannah , Savannah air until Dallas.
I will never jet over south east asia wastes & jungles I never want to.

*

O'hara died like christ
a blue chrysler struck him down
he died suddenly in a field of white yellow daisies
scattered among grass, he died surreally
in a kitchen wallpaper

he had fallen off a stepladder
awkwardly rehearsing his death
                        a daisy
grew among his teeth and one
curved up his ass curiously orphic
he lay there dead hands extended into another life

he might have fallen off a ladder hanging wallpaper
on a Bucks County ceiling
pushed away and twisted to his death
one star torn from a blue mural, bothering
to lightly descend upon his head.

I doubt several friends of his were there
innocently playing with him after
a blue chrysler had tapped the life from him;
I doubt they realized he could be dead
having arrived at a death so ineffectually
that no one had bothered to arrange a thunderstorm
and sandpipers didn't shriek their brains out
for this crushed gentle poet

who turned as he died away from the car
or possibly rolled away after the wheels
had contracted his chest and arm;
I doubt anybody knew what he was doing
when he silently tumbled down to earth.

God's love on tenderness, the harbormaster
of Long Island Sound gone
to sleep.

*

1947

Something must be said about the others born 1947. if you yourself were not, we can tell you roughly this. 1947 threw up the years around it and spasms and retches still reach out everyway. it was the year that was ashamed; the year that hid its children in serious amphetamine serious meditation serious consideration of the request — bequest of the mothering years. the year that looked at what expensive parties were being thrown at what would be held up to later years without any shame presented as something dying and a thing worth saving yet, not worth the effort of an unthrown party. they hid in an opaque metaphor that was disgust before laughter. they spent time with the absurd sum of what once was. they were serious about living away from that. they were concerned with directions. no energy was theirs from that year to engage life with. perhaps it was this; they threw up that. you can't walk up to 1947 with any deception though. they are the ones who stood still to watch to throw up and to laugh seriously. don't look for us between ages; we can walk alongside even between years but we have nothing to contribute, except to perhaps be seen re-enacting the pageant of the throwing-up.

*

There are a thousand parts of travelling
long distances
there is a sphere of bus-schedule
informations, more,
the exact routes cities bypassed the
statement of wealth Trailways displays in Chicago
but in Chicago I didn't get the city feeling
when you pass by bus you pass right thru
every city is/becomes an amen of
the massed fragments
o Christ we will have travelled
be still travelling, upon death.

*

Frank O'hara

Frank O'hara
          how did you hold out
with your sensitivities against you
only useful to your poetry
which was written at home anyhow?

Frank O'hara
               they must have bustled
you, and yelled loudly at you till
your delicate ear and tongue
froze with a fear and a horror for life

          or till a younger boy crept
passed you with locks of delicate hair
and eyebrows like
                    licorice icing
how Frank how?

          I see you as a target
for deadly parties
                    where the voices
were tinged with vodkas
                    coloured
with bright syrups
                    like in a court
presided over by poets, and plotting ministers
such as critics are
                    and are
the ungenteel of this life.

and of course you are in some flitty heaven
where pictures are shuffled
as in exhibitions
of the men you chose to love, and wheel past you
delicately whatever happened in your life

wheeled past you delicately
while you presided
in pansy court, but Frank
you showed them what was real

*

In the scheme of things perfectly contained the poet is a spy, a wriggling.
perfect perhaps is the stillness of the small peasant fisherman who on a
willow pattern chintz drops his quiet line over a bridge and forever fishes.
The poet shouts foul the poet sighs beautiful perfect but will not shut up.
The poet needs to tell the universe to the blue & white Nanking fisherman.
When the fisherman looks up at the poet and smiles, then the balloon he is is
tugged and he may haul up the struggling poet the struggling drowning man up
from the flowing river water to where the sun will in a while place a gentle
hand over the twitching gills of the poet.   he only wants too much white oxygen.
content after tasting it each time to lapse among the cool bone china glaze.

*

'The trouble with comparing' yer life to a ballgame
is that a dead fool will have no obituary, but a ball
even when lobbed shows a token
amount of revolution. The trouble
is the hotdogs and whatnots we treat ourselves to
extemporaneously. The trouble is one of

demonstrating suitable analogy; we
endure only once. The trouble is the tragedy
that even well chosen, our analogy will not delay a game
indefinitely.
              The trouble is popcorn vendors
and game officials. The question becomes one
of recourse, and here, even heroes
show unimpressive scores.

The trouble with contesting
is that in life we are constantly outcontested
constantly unaware of our being outcontested. The trouble
with belief in this and in experience is that it comes
as intellectual sentiment, and is never useful to us
when a shut-out has already decided th game. Baseball
is still interesting carried passed
the second inning.

                    — *after Spicer*

                              *

Sun filters through my window
velvet like bats' bellies the shadows it casts
flutter about my room. I share the unrest

the sun is doomed with; the movement
sunup sundown moving around: ground sky ground
its only comfort the habit of its orbit.

we are orbs whatever we do is behaviour
the truth of our moment is too predictable
yet I delight in the sun. it is monumental

in the sky with certainty rising, setting
looking to the greater cycle, there is colour,
a yellow angel pedals about the world.

*

J: I am Jack Spicer inventor of language
     my lemons are such as you would want
     to find on any lemon tree.

F: I am Frank O'hara sensitive to the perception
     of things visual and abstracted.

J: I died after 40 days of coma
     I broke free to follow a muse
     at the speed of my heart.

F: I was killed in what was described as tragedy
     a car driven by friends drove me to this place
     there were fields of daisies in the grass I lay down in
     my sleep was short like Rousseau's poet asleep or
     even that of Chagall's. I awoke bruised at the foot
     of the ladder I'd stumbled from.

J: To you will always be the task of reading
     the scrollwork on the casket's side.

F: It is rather like the lines of Pollock, tho
     nothing could ever be qualified.

J: I watched them bury me perfume me from their sense of decay
     I was pointed northwards like a magnetized needle.

F: And I, like a homing bird did fly steadily
     towards a line
     seagulls ignored as if it did not exist —
     I had imagined there was a harbor there
     a medieval harbor the restless ship of soul
     could forever have arrived at
     to travel no more.

J: I see a harbor, at Amsterdam, perhaps, the harbormaster
     has hung a plague sign from the mast; an incoming ship
     would be wise to pass on to another sanctuary.

F:	A coloured harbor where disease has marked the faces of the sailors
ghostly pale and cut up, teredos have burrowed through their skins.

J:	A teredo as real as greyish-fleshy-pink, a teredo, moored at one end
the other wriggling as though life itself were an agony.

F:	That swimming away from, cannot even stretch the distance an inch
whose source of energy of current were to be found by burrowing
in that same direction the agony is fed from.

J:	There are tides of life; currents of life; biogenic
senses of life; that move us with the sense of basic purpose.
There are no sides to no bathtub
we are involved in
the fulfilment of
natural tendencies.

F:	Life is the blue streak that is undeniable, life
is life energy. Jane and I, in a canoe.

J:	All, is hunter and food, all we are all our lifetimes
are nomads who wander to taste
an illusionary change in soil. Lawnmowers are so useless when
one cutting of our lawns and
a different need for territory arises.

F:	Charon or some bastard fires arrows at us
to speed life so fast, not even if we found an easier path to death
would it be feasible. There was no satisfaction in dying so suddenly
had I even willed it to be, it did not come as any answer, rather
too quick a surprise even to be
remarked upon.

J:	The birds are determined to survive in their flight. They wing
through empty space, connecting no two points together, and yet
their determination is so strong as not only to define a mission
but also to realize death as happening, only after,
some more important conclusion has passed in their lives.

F: I can only see the paths they make. no space lies in their ways that is in any way defined. They seem aimless, this one, that one, until they occur at what they are doing. They are enclosed in a frame that is inches short of encompassing life itself. Their lives and their deaths too, seem those of waiting, their frame gives them no recourse at all. They are merely doomed with an excess of velocity — so they continue to fly.

J: The restingplace of god exists in those edges, those small corners that encompass the frame they fly in. Occasionally, one is guided by the voice of a muse or crack of light reflected, directly from the eye of god, occasionally one strays outwards, with greater destination. A bird received an olive branch from outside, and moses travelled in the same bird's eyes to view the land his feet could never touch. A dove will light upon the eye or nose of god and be photographed there a million times a second; will bathe in the warm light of god's face and remain transfixed there, for a million years until the smile has grown brighter, and the bird has been absorbed. The controls of love and time and rain, are hidden inside god's fleshy face like the cone, cotton candy is swirled about. To gaze upon the face of god is disbelief or utter relief.

F: I can see birds glance off the edges of the sky. I cannot see the end of the blue, I'm sure goes on forever.

J: Forever is an adverb, may be dispensed with if considered simply a vast space of time. Perhaps a lifetime, even greater, but must end must terminate in the place of its generation. The machine which is constantly creating sky and clouds, is the muscle of god's power is the source and the continuation of every cycle. An anger in the machine may destroy a continent or cast a dark hole in the sky. God seems to be directly available as a wall ships and birds cannot easily pierce. God is the hand that catches the ship or bird that departs at all horizons at once.

F: And is as symmetrical as a golfball in a vacuum. Though there is no
       perception, no visualizing what you say.

J: God is what makes itself live, god is time caught, arrested, to be taken
       home bottled in a jar; to be explored at the leisure of unended life.
       God is the emancipation. that must be attained. God is the renewing
       wish of life; god is the expansion of sensation. You must strive to
       avail yourself of god's own organs and you will be small god, also
       contained in the space of that bottle. in the space of a point where
       all that is tasted expands about you and
       lingers.

F: The edges of my picture. birds fly   within and are contained in
       the spaces and junctures my neck will always bend in, travelling
       alongside my infinitely expanding body. My enlightenment is a parallel
       successive burgeoning of my body. The blind spot my vision will never
       contain, has travelled infinitely outwards where, it is an infinitely
       more accessible annoyance. O, that I were point from which to search.

J: And harbor too is parallel. All achievement and expectation mimic
       the tiny human body. Vast cartoons exist in death, where senses may
       fly unhampered outwards, undisturbed by the immediacy of real action.
       Life's misconceptions are towed with unaffordable luxury into waters
       where heaviness is felt directly, many times more intense. Error
       is magnified by weightlessness.

F: And poetry

J: was why/you were never a painter! ! !

F: And it was compulsive feeding of
       a hideous waistline which ignored
       both greed of time and logic.   And yet
       was my only voice — the piece of curtain
       I had borrowed from god
       to cry tears of the play onto. And in a single day
       I was dead, while all my life I battled headwinds to reach
       a place of solace, truly belonging to me.
       It was my harbor master —

J: And it was constantly destroyed by the pirates that prevail
     on the seas of the winds; the imagination sets sail on
     so recklessly in its own
     Caribbean.

F: And whom have you to discuss any success or failure with?
     There cannot be so hideous a Sunday afternoon as you — so
     sorry a man who knew and yet still
     was not the master of just one lifetime?

J: I was born before I was born
     only fairies and grail-carriers
     did comfort me second time coming: I was more
     of a vision, and yet: more of a real life-spirit
     and was torn apart battling my own body
     that threatened to die in San Francisco.

     Crop failures would be the fate of any man who planted
     in the seasons of the god.
     Death occurred to harvest
     wheat human purpose thought to reap;
     that the fields combed from
     the fleece of god's own body
     could ever grow wild or disorderly
     with such strivings.
     My battle against myself bruised my body
     slammed down on it by my other hands that
     were god wielded and sought and did indeed
     destroy with such a thoroughness
     unintended for the wounds to be
     left on human body.

F: Jack, your body has been twisted from the earth
     and you are dead in bathtubs with
     burst heart and eyeballs! !

J: And repentance of a type is achieved, now that I may freely
       come and go. The edge of lenses cannot
       reflect shadow on the clear
       viewing of baseball or poems
       (If I choose them too
       about baseball.

F: Jackson stretches from a ghost-car windshield
       to paint the cotton candy tarpaulin our entrance has unlifted.
       There is as much chance/as ever for us.

                              *

Sometimes as if life itself were the enemy
I pelt myself with pills to slow it down
My face bends itself to launch itself into
a wind of arrows and through sheer
perseverance I climb to craggy lofts
  higher than 5 fools   from amphetamine
mountain   I shake my fist
  at a world past seeing

*

EVEN YR PHOTOGRAPH LOOKS AFRAID OF ME

for Mary

Don't Stop Clapping Till I'm Famous . . .

It was the greatest poetry reading Canada ever heard
AJM Smith was there with his polaroid land camera
Earle Birney stood by the door flipping his lucky

both-sides beaver nickel

The Governor-General smiled like a Parisian-born trick
you could hear everywhere hoofbeats of moose & windblown birch boughs
Everyone was related to everybody else.
Across the audience smiles broke like quebec bridges
I kept thinking the face on the very next guy to read was the
splitting image of an autumn-blown maple leaf atop Mount Royal
we threw the critics out early in the show
they asked the poets the wrong kind of questions and we just knew
they'd leave early and cause trouble for us

/ at the banks)

famous people read aloud and no smart-asses coughed at crucial points
the concluding speech told you what the next fifty years of canadian
poetry would be like, whereupon
All stood
And the flag
was raised & lowered by the unseen hands
of Robert Service's ghost who'd been with us since intermission
I was proud
alka-seltzer-proud . . .

a patriot was stationed at each exit and it was the patriot's duty
to after each poet had read / fling open the door to the subzero howling
winds which beat at all our faces and cold that turned the sweat on our
cheeks to icicles / while a sign was held up above the stage's dais which
read:

> DON'T STOP CLAPPING FOR A MINUTE FOLKS
>   OR YOU'LL NEVER HOLD ANOTHER PENCIL BETWEEN
>   YOUR FROSTBITTEN FINGERS

— thank you,
— merci.

Look,
when an elm leaf scoops empty baskets of air
emptying them out on either side and drifts down
and dies
I think it's Bartok
and wonder if canada ought to have solid hitting poetry
because its maple leaves come down with a whoppe
but then figure not everything hammers into my country like blows, no,
snow flakes individually dance sparkle in the same sun that sets
on senegal and the senegalese so please please don't feed me bunk
about how canadian my poetry oughta be, mister.

Canada First

I was about to slip into something comfortable (like NBC movie of
                                                        the week
but flipping through channels saw this ad flash on my screen
it said: see *Canada First*! (well I thought

            ok
and slipped into my study where I just happened
to have a copy on hand.
I read it carefully cover-to-cover
I was getting confused. I found nothing
and I was missing the first part of "I WAS CURIOUS, GEORGE"/
the part where they tell you what will happen at the end of the movie

it was a government sponsored message though
and I'm a better Canadian than the next guy) —
so I thought I'd better phone someone and ask what they meant by ". . .
    SEE *CANADA FIRST*."
so after being told by a pretty, recorded voice that
Information Canada's office hours were 9am to 5pm/
I thought it was high time I called a friend
and got the matter straightened out (
Mannix with guest star Joe Dallesandro
    was on in 6 minutes!

AM I STUPID!
(that's what my friend kept saying to me)
"THEY MEAN THAT YOU SHOULD SEE
    THE *COUNTRY*
CANADA FIRST!!!!!

(why before Mannix, I thought . . . ?
  maybe it was a campaign
to show the people
that Canada was as good as any American t.v. detective show.

I was on my second cup of coffee. It was a long night . . . the buses
were all on strike that week
so it wasn't before 4am that I'd changed my typewriter ribbon,
                                        grabbed a spare/
and was finally on my way down L'Acadie
towards Metropolitan to the trans
Canada interchange. WHAT A NIGHT OF HECTIC DRIVING
I COULD HARDLY SEE ANYTHING IT WAS SO DARK
                                        AROUND KINGSTON.
my typewriter and I were exhausted. I parked outside the N.C.R.
Building in downtown Kingston and after locking it
   vowed tomorrow and all subsequent days
    to drive only during daylight hours/since
SEEING CANADA, first meant
having my eyes OPEN
and I'm a good Canadian (better than most . . . and
I DON'T LOOK FOR LOOPHOLES
AND EASY WAYS TO GET OUT OF DOING MY PATRIOTIC DUTY
    and most drivers get
   a bit reckless
     trying to pass me/
on my right hand shoulder.
                        (drat this / overhead-steering!).

I near got botulloid scampi brought
before me (I swear on the maple leaf
the thing on my plate had fight in it yet!)

the moth sound asleep in the plastic clear
forehead of the jukebox
is the brains,
the total brains behind
this management   pay when served;
Rather should the sign have read: PAY
AS YOU EAT!!!

The Pumpkin Eaters

Oh Canada . . . Let me count the ways!
he's the new King of Israel (what a movie!
Can't think what I might ask him
except perhaps if the 'o' of 'of' is to be capitalized.
When you beat me up oh Canada . . .
A last desperate attempt to sell me beer
over the television. wait. let me get my glasses.
why it's gone now! why did you make me
go through all this rigmarole for later of fuck-all?
Deep are your ways, Oh Canada, long are your days
and you deign to let me sit on your lap!
Dazzling. dazzling. I swear by parliament
Your come is my immediate heartburn, birch
Your incisors bite my back like all the
beavers born and died since 1534.

'Oak-Canada'? no — wouldn't be the same: Oh
Canada . . . keep it simple (painful) always maple!
Oh Canada, when you beat me up in your alleys,
I go black & blue on you, become gradually —
The Archbishop of Canadian Surrealism (— Oh Canada . . .)
what a movie! Even New Brunswick
has its finger up my ass!

Cochon

The farmer of your tongue is
growing poets for the cities
paying off th loan with pig-poems
so slickers keep hating th country
paying fancy pork prices.
already half New York's waiters
are model french *garçons*,
paying to be treated poorly in Paris;
get homesick, addicted to the talking tourist
ejected bodily from Berlitz
by an elderly jewish school teacher from Colorado
who wouldn't ease the reins; working that frog to death.

Why didn't you come? vacation! *congé*!
why didn't you stay? didn't you
                              like it?
                    : yougottalemmebackin: —
                    Ahm an American!!!

The fools of Gotham
Ambassadors of war
bubblegum, baseball,
bringing hongkong flu
home on a fast jet.

Ultra Modern Times

in ultra modern times
you say, hand me   that plastic
    or this plastic   or that plastic
it suddenly isn't crucial
    McGovern wins the democratic nomination
    no one rides through Montreal shouting
The Americans are coming!
The Americans are coming!

But the Americans   are coming

in ultra modern times
you've got to plan a product
    to seem suddenly wonderful tomorrow
    to seem as though it might last forever
you have to be ultra sneaky
    and give them different reasons
when you come across the border.

Inform the General

Inform the general
we are about to leave
inform the general his jeep
drives over my foot
the maidens are cowardly
there is nothing left but whole wheat
fire engines are red
there is no enemy in this country
inform the general
of the winter retreat
of the general conditions
that the men have no cotton batting
that their wounds are festering
that the other army's strongest
we have killed the pope
inform the general.

"I used to live   in New York City
                       everything there
    was dark
    and dirty"

but this doesn't matter if
the Puerto Rican junkies
don't knife you down
                       it was more of a struggle
to stay alive/happiness
never occurs to bother you
when you are struggling
just to stay alive.

it's only when I think of the churches
and the taverns Montreal has
then Montreal is suddenly
too far north — we can't
use a city this cold.) — besides
I'm not benefiting
I'm not benefiting.

I used to think when I lived in New York City
an angel might come   or
money could make it better   and magic
happens in these
crowded cities:
magic happens.

                  it was more of a struggle
        than even a dream. I used to dream of a dollar thrown
        across the Potomac
                       with me on its back
        to New Jersey. The Potomac was the East
        River,   but then
I was willing
to travel further.
                  "Outside my window was a seagull."

and an eagle,
an important eagle.
                    (it was just a big
building. It was just
a big buildup).

The old stores of this neighborhood
I remember how well served
I was   never had to go out but
half a block
in any
direction from my
                              flat / then
  down came every last one of them
  I remember
    everything
everything
as I light my last pallmall   & bicycle
                                    to another city/
the cars, 2-to-a-lot
looking like farmers

     doing
something someone from duplexes
cannot identify out of sidewindows
    lost
  yet
        somehow very large
  standing occupying every farflung
clover swatch, clumps of this, bushes
  or a solitary bottlecap, as little as that to
break the snooze of the tarmac stretching out from
                                        under a buick
              /whose colour
                I hardly notice, whose chrome shines
    more for Detroit than for people.
unquestionably , the owner of the city
      certainly the "Giant" in a fairy tale
one to a lot (one beanstalk one cloud
      one empty, lonely city
parking
          free   downtowns
          on Sundays).

we will visit a few towns
we will look for unusual
                    symptoms
we will drink coca-cola
with the natives, leaning our elbows
on their spangled formica
and see what this will tell us

we will approach their state capitals
in broad daylight   and our cars will
carry more than adequate papers
and we will never be very far
        from our cars
we will never leave our cars
unlocked   but
    we will never leave our necessary
    papers, locked in our glove-dash compartments

if people ask us why we really
drove our bodies so far southwards
    because, we will tell them in Atlanta
    the magnolias are more beautiful in winter.

Waiting for a 36 Bus in Berkeley

Suddenly   I

    lookup   and   try   to   grasp

 a   star

     in   my   fist

while

    the   young   boy's

    transistor   radio   has   me

    dancing   uncontrollably!

The heart's ability to push the
mileage back on a rental
Trying is not essential
time goes towards love's labor
and wasted words
tower over finished poems.
Days: a string of visits to the world;
Worth, seen in a string of visit after visit,
re-entering the island experiences that made us
resent the staying in Montreal til each of us in
turn/had his childhood dream/
flip us out, watching for some reason
to be intentionally terrified.
we had nightmares our bodies older than the ancientest sea tortoise
in blue detroit aquariums that slowly cruised into surgery
where artists labored into the small morning hours in mirrors
to restore the paint that falling away
let the cold winter light in.

There are two poems exactly alike.
poem one is a surrealist poem in which
each chamber (full or empty) of
Mayakovsky's revolver   lobbies for 1 of 2
tenses to be applied to Mayakovsky's compulsion
in a poem where it may linger (M.'s
being dead-on-demand / or reproduceable
at all points within the poem : alive, still.
A poem can happen in real life until
it engages surrealism. Surrealist poems
tear (an act) apart   into 1st part when
nothing has happened and nothing suggests
it (any specific thing) ever will happen   in such way that the
2nd part, perfectly-is-that act, having
lived, its purpose always there (so implicitly
that) births of 2 types of chambers (with & without
bullets) would be un-understandable
and not important but for full chamber.
An empty bullet chamber always pointed
at Mayakovsky's head — each-minute —
of his life — from birth till his death. a
constantly (surrealism is wise) unsuccessful murdering
until one day (any day after) the bullet is finally come
surrealism is people seeing that bullet (year after year)
inching down an almost   endless barrel's length.

I pluck a tear off on the end of my finger
and I dial it on my jeans
I am reading Simenon
he writes too human . . .
it is dawn   6:15 perhaps
2 seagulls   cruise suspended in the sky
on their under bellies   on their wings   orange glints
That is all.

across from where I am
lights turn on in   apartment kitchenettes
three floors off the ground, the regulars
their windows mylar palest apricot
off to work
back almost at dusk
gone too early
lights turned off   asleep not late enough
their windows hang
silver mica   against the pale evening.

Sometimes I think I have
worked myself down deep
in a mine   that I have
caved in   the shoring behind me
that for 4 years
life has been such an intense
hell I am now
unable at all to scream
unable in any way to signal to
some somebody who may be on
the outside
where there is air
where a mountain
does not sit on my chest
where the heavy squeeze
                          of hell
does not pin me
under a pressure
of a thousand oceans
  all coming down on me
some someone I hope will
suddenly appear when swinging
through that last rock encumbrance
let in the air of the world   rush in and save me
let me after a forever out of this hell I have
secured myself in in only
4 short
years of poetry.

The coffee's not made yet
the water's playin Happy Trails . . .
I've gulped down so many pills
      these last two days / noises
  are coming outamyhead;

In third and fourth person my lost thoughts
sneak over my shoulder
              into my head again
burn little messages of recognition in.

What needs doing / in my life
seems determined to recapture me
then like friendly blackmail

oversee to it — that the lad
lay down equal hours
in gusting it along sober —

If it doesn't serve him well
at least   it'll serve him right.

I sometimes park my convertible along the curb,
hours early across the street from my muse's house
and cannot honk my claxton & call her out yet
so I sit hunched up/my elbow under my chin
Inside enough energy to roar across a continent
It's as if I were the discus thrower of the greeks
Squeezed into the body of Rodin's Thinker
or *perhaps I am standing before a chest of drawers*
as if it were a one-armed bandit somewhere in
                                        Las Vegas
I cannot put my money in, even to lose it
and wonder if my poem even if it turns out
good this once, is worth the effort of those
                                other times.

The poem I am writing
is Charles Ives, standing thinking
his second Piano Sonata

    this is moving from him in its performance

there is little else of this piece
   he has left others to fuddle with;
just the gentle old man
thinking and humming
beside a piano river .

The piano is the poem itself, not
an instrument of background
if there were to be a landscape
with the river a single line on it,
maybe a rag doll , with the patches
blown up to be separate fields
and farms .
he plays it in Bucks County,
for it seems to me and him
that America
    happened most there .

Difficult Sonnet

The first energy
       elegy is to say
physics isn't alive
      isn't as
versatile as a dead poet.
Things with histories
are casually written off.
We can afford time
we jingle our pockets
               and jingling
is rhyming.
         but we cannot
         two-time
         what avails us
not.

*

The second
       elegy is a warning
as all elegies are
our own source
of remorse. We only
write of things/we loved
that died/that's
not right
       (it makes us rather
up tight
at times.

       I counted twenty
       tragedies
       on twenty toes
       then couldn't go on
       (but then I dreamed
        that I was dreaming.
and I awoke
broke.

*

You were dreaming too
                    is the third elegy
dreaming about dying and falling
like supportless
dangling necks —
what the heck
            or
what the heck, what's next
                        or
what's it
to me ?
            I could have told you you were safe with me, my fly
            had jammed on an upstroke, broke as it were.

                    *

Go to Iowa you'll see brass statuary
of famous men who first conceived
of ever stopping there.
                    Mostly cornfields
                    and corn
                    flakes.
                            (though they have a way
of keeping the dead among
the living. this is
                the magic
                of the unimaginative).
Iowa is little less
than a proverb/Chicago
would be the verb in this case.)

You may as well eat wheaties
and support champions.

                    *

You could survive/as well
the place is ideal as setting
for surreal novels in which
hurricanes
or tornadoes
could occur
                    (picking Kansas, Frank L. Baum
was only exercising
extreme caution.
                    The hero could sit
                    on a tall stalk of corn
                    exercising his perogative
                    while scaring crows
                    with his bent yellow weapon.

surreal novels
are hardly necessary
except as fuel
for the hardy.

                              *

Soup every day
makes a
soupy-er you
                    Here the source of ready-made confusion
                    seems to be ready made
                    syllables

or proverbs they distend
to throw back at us)
soup
for elegies.

                              *

gullible
syllables   in search
            of relevance. relieve
the language through
awkward
mannerisms —
womanerisms?

but then people still achieve
glacial ignorance in Mantaqua
, Long Island.
            because you can't fool
            a fool
                 ,   (you may as well
not try.

                         *

to some people being lost
is far more frightening than
being wrong, though
they amount to
the same
            a strong image
            creating fear
                    (if I hadn't told you you were supposed
                        to fear
                            you might have merely
got lost.

Pome for Virgins and Dreamers

I have plied my typewriter
but it is a drunken rock
late Wednesday's poetry
is improper (or
improbable.
            as I am using red-
red ink
       I can fight the polar nature of Malachite.
       To make a poem proper in form
        it must be true
to life.

Drunken medicine men
8 letters, no further clues
fit it in
a cross word puzzle.
Drunken medicine men
shamans with silver
heavy chains
and single-eyed
malachites. and through the night
she sits
       at my right, fitting
colored paper scraps
on a white back-
ground.

      I ought to poke her eyes out
of her eye-sockets
they cannot be similar
but these are topazes
and are not in polar
juxtaposition.
just suppose
we were medicine
          men

not shams
and it wasn't
an improper
        Wednesday night
suggestion.

"Why you kid
        I oughta . . . (but
I withdraw
  sleepily
and park my dreamy body
beside this drunken red pen
the point was hardly worth
its nature —
        hardly green
in this dream, though cozy —
when is Wednesday night-
Thursday morning?
hardly ever.
Hardly ever at 12:00,
perhaps at 4:30.
A poem could be written in two days
in one sitting
if you ignored
the green inner clock
        (mobius surface
of th next day. I
have little to say/
I am not your father —

I would rather be crazy
if it entitled me
to a better position.
I would issue rain dances at you
and frighten you, Bob,
        with
    gestures
from crazy fingers; you'd say

If you'd rather be crazy than be
my father — then
you're crazy!
                    And
I'd sit back
abandoning my drunken rock
and regard you
        with one eye
one
        non-Euclidean eye
that hadn't any converse
and spit red   .
at your young green
nature visions.
Consider the tomato
a death-defying experience
as it enters your world
contemplate

a death-defying experience
as it enters your world.
contemplate lobsters, etc.

Eat a few tomatoes
yer green, Bob,
                    you, Dave,
are also the kind of virgin
that rejects anything that isn't green. You never
drink red wine with
the girls that you fuck.

If a poem is true,
        forms,
    probable images
      or image
and is ultimately
        acceptable in your eyes —
consider only what is spoken
Will you disregard those things you think
you could safely spend a night with.

at 4:30/th morning
climb to conclusions
aspire to be loved and only enter
mountains your eyes have first climbed
your women have no staircases inside of them
their bodies could be filled
with human effort

                    but I
will throw tomatoes at you
buy you red wine
and cherries
                    (and teach you
Dharma, then you can stand
at the threshold of your women
and fully enter them.

Phrase Book

there is too much wrong with this soup for me to accept it

the women of the city break my heart

I know I will always be a foreigner

I would rather be rolling in your arms now
than watching Mannix.
I would rather be caught
with a stolen Rembrandt than be caught
playing 'Krazy' to your 'Ignatz' another night.
O exploring th heartache
I am a blind sexual
blunderer.

We ride tandem together squeezed to fit so snugly
unromantic analogy of my being the lightbulb
that your current finds release through
makes me giggle lift my head up towards you . . .
It would be fantastic: — to see you smile too.

The Week's Dirty Poem

when life is an Indian attack
you come like the Cavalry
remember your saying to me
I'll come over only on the
condition that
after
you had left
I remember wondering to myself
what just what
that condition
could possibly have been

really now

there you were stretched out on top of me
everything you did
everything you said
only
served to get me twice as excited
you said
so you like having your ass played
with, eh? yes,
god yes, I said,
don't stop doing exactly what you're doing
You wish you could be fucked by a horse I'll bet
that's exactly what you told me
and I remember thinking god this
broad wishes she could be fucked by a horse
and using it to get home on

Calendars
        are very much
like Snakes & Ladders
                Tomorrow
has no monopoly
on our lives. Days
are great transvestites, or perhaps
the clothing worn
to an expensive restaurant.

                To say
I cannot wait to see
my Jeanie, O
I cannot wait
to see my
Jean/is like a big lie
no one will hang you for.
what you mean really
is that
        you could wait months
or even years
and be satisfied if
even Susan
turned up tomorrow
to let you have it.
              Calendars
are the bar-30 brand
that's slaked across my logic
and weekends are a lot more
like rodeos/than riding range, heaven

is a tumble
weed thrown to us
by Spanish priests
who wear long black
suffering looks/and robes
that cowboys would feel
awkward in
and stumble off their horses
in the darkness
of that tricky footwork.

It's like putting yer head in a bag
and riding round Manhattan
how do you manage?

She'll say I try
and keep busy all the time

But in the thirties
Pound and them
traded perceptions by mail!

Then she'd have no answer
perhaps it's closer to the truth
when we meet a day later

all those things we didn't say last nite
perhaps could wait forever.

Then suddenly an idea
might strike me on the forehead.

You know when we talk about god and space and all those things?
Yeah!   Yeah well
think about me.

Psycho

For years I've been sharing showers
with women too afraid to shower alone

— well, since about '1965' anyhow . . .)

— lucky for them, Hitchcock,
    that I'm around/ I mean,

— we might really've
    had a problem on our hands, eh?

We Counted the Ways

We counted the ways   on a scale, nothing short of shameless / for
the better part of 3 days
stopping only to palaver
   at the refrigerator (2 ways to eat
   and maybe more, if you're well connected)
      and plug a nosebleed up witha snatch of cotton, twisted;
         should we in our money-house
            sink our teeth down on some strange   new coin
            whose alloy backfired into
               our physical bodies lying together
            on the mattress like lewd barbie&Ken dolls
grinning at the next thing we'd hike
               our average up with
         before the dogwork of the actual doing

      but so we wldn't lose
         a second's loving
            the cuckold baked bean qt-jar w/
            the cotton baton caulking, lay
         at the most an only ½-inconveniencing
                     backhand arms-grasp from us/
            (not really enuff to more than only
               sway   the spiderwebbings we acted out, very greatly;
         indebted to the thread of
slender liquid silk coming in the long run from
                     geometric Saxon
                     /body precision
         . . . to/ 'Heidegger-variable' mind-singing-(about
sans foot, somewheres in that   vast sexual sea &
                              forest
            /indeterminate composite of
         haunting lostness

and   we   came   until   we   had   to   stop
                  (for fear of a neighbor's concerned
            shot at the phone's worst wld be done & down upon
               us wld suddenly from nowhere swoop the bombsquad

                    to test the bedroom
                    for guncotton smell
                 is there a sexual
                breath test used, I wonder,
             by field raids of morality officers
                working on the road ironing & starchstraight fixing
                      by ad hoc maintenance, appearance's
                 to cull greater self-percentages from
                 everyday way of debaucheries idolatry ?
                 I do believe
                    there is
                            furthermore
                 it is like there even/   :ARE;

each of us   unbending   to relax
body,   limp as jello only shouts itself suitable to so demonstrate,
          oh waves passing over our tight seconds at the zenith of sex
             were six cannon broadsides leveled at our boat-bows before
finally deciding to finish the marionettes dance act borderstript
bareass naked to jolts of wilhelm reichish rakish-psychosexual/registry
all I was sure of was that it might be snowing my alpha patterns
in a blizzard that whitened everything but the golden curls sworle

      oh we were sun-baked
                         jamaican tourists
             on a hot beach
                             that skirted the mexican blue waters
      a pacific bracelet, the path of a finger described along naked back
             as softly as the birds see the sunset of colours
             in the air through which they still sweep
             unconscious of the blue's infected eye-glow.

      10 years before god created the winds   place of stillness
of perfect   it was far back enough to settle down to the
      peace /   business of the comfort we were about.

      high on every drug shot through every arm
             as often as effective as powerful as being led
      to die through a backwards path that sees first our selves
      once more born uncomplicatingly inwound around

                              98

the pleasure maypole of pagan passion
top note struck on some cock-stavian scale of soul-music
a new allowance under the old limits of physical world's
                                relaxation, come;
double doing it like siamese twins with a common
    brain that filled so full it was a veritable cesspool of
lowmorality filled with lover's hi-fidelity
                                whenever together doing it;
there are cried Cantor the mathematician, incidentally
    quite correctly; always (here I paraphrase him slightly), better
                ways to begin to get high   and   these ways
        followed to culmination through serial titillation of
        all known ordinates' co-operation, will followed through
    bring the pencil scratcher to a better peace with the greater itch
under the old method of scratching, unreachable, too inaccessibly SINFUL

            chalk up Dr Kinsey 10 points more for canada
            & look around other places than suburban New Jersey
                        for the mouths of your sources
                    when recording record lengths, loves)
    you see I take the Houston Avenue express
    nonstop all the way to Coney Island
    whatsmore I get there faster than my chick so therefore
    like it all the more left with NO OTHER CHOICE BUT to
                            wait   for/her, do you
                            begin to see Dr. skinZ:
never however even for a second do I abandon
    position about her taken like a poll
        strategic to   the way the mattress rolls when we really get GOING
I wonder if sometime it isn't the salt & pepper literature&lubricants
        stationed beforehand for our convenience & added chance of deviance
            up on the ledge above our heads that are kissing faster
            than heads of bantams cockfighting with the will to live
                        the real spur spurring them
                        into so dizzying a flurry
    that extra little something I can't seem to keep from snacking upon

did we open Pandora's box just when she'd finished putting into stock
the latest inverse perversions twisted fresh from ripe *thou/musn'ts*)

someone twice as kittenish as the pope's lengthiest litanies are long
must want us to come to town with an empty basket to start picnic
                                                        gossip —
pass the leg I say to her one foolishly indulgent last time & out
go the juices half drowning me in inner-battery causing to me joy
    that hurts me when it is because its strings are my lungs' undoings
        what goes on god this has got to stop are you still
                            there honey (I worry because when I pinch myself
    I'm heavy again her near total fluid weight, having swallowed
    enough for the poor dear's brain's hydrolysis.

            and all she manages was a slight hissss and
                I'm not sure at all that it was her that I was hearing
one mad thought before I go under for a week of recovering normalcy
is I can't wait to get to the point where again we may go off again
                                                        from,
    clam up bitch, I dream, the
    seafood's certainly
        excellent
            here . . . weirdness for the critics
who are secret moral puritans (the one thing I can't stand
    to see my purity soiled by — give me rather a

                        smuttiness of muse-caliber, juices of the soul's water
and take it up like something automatic, overfishing; like the
        whistle of wire-thinness the air bores into through & jets-out
    when the swallow sweeps over a lake picking up breathtaking speeds
        and is any other way than drilling for air with its body, unable to
keep conscious & coming round graceful the curve's bends without
    the gills of fishes or something else too awkward to conceive of
        being used in swimming through   the thin blue seas
        before the eyes all the eternity of daytimes bringtogether.

SHE WORRIES   — when I sleep a three day
stretch awake and then,
sleep another three day stretch and THEN I STAY AWAKE a full
Seven days (now this has her something more than worried —
she didn't even believe th thing possible — and I say to her — look —

how am I going to ever be mad if I can't practice
and she is horrified by th silliness
Is it common then, I ASK, for a human being to write poems? HUH?

NUMEROUS CUT UP dirty books lie strewn throughout my room
I am going to make the dirtiest book of them all and this will not
even have redeeming literary graces
it will turn young ladies grape-cheeked
their mouths agaped and wondering finally
what the point of clothes was. O YES,
Dirty Indeed
Twill Be!

There will be no opportunity for
excuses from enemies of the state
postmasters will instantly resign
and critics will withhold erections
from the curious waiting public.
DIRTY indeed.

mischief

with a touch   less   grand eloquence

will cure my poems

will make

my poems

be well again

, I wrote. with even just

a pinch   less meat

in them

your meatloafs

wld just loaf

, I laughed as I bit into

yer waldorf-salad

which survived

vast onion drifts

with no beef

to guide them
                    thru
the arctic night

of your 450 degree

cooking spree.

There are areas where my mother
was uncompromisable — for instance
if she had used Ben's instead of
Dainty rice as she had — perhaps
our lives would have been happier

then there were the meatloafs.
they were good. but you couldn't touch them.
there were the scenes, scenes where she
broke down completely, the locked doors, the sobbing:
You children ruined my life, because of you
I can never marry. but weren't you married once?

is once not enough for you?
dear mother
I would not
live *my* life over. not
for anything in this
world!

See what they can take from
us to pay the organist for his
not breaking into open laughter
seeing our pride in paying to shovel
over our dear dead dad,
what kills me is the man's
cashier, working by mail,
can buy the beach
                from under our feet
and good at his job an organist
adds a dignity for those to whom
death and the coffin being
left open
                /have as little meaning
to the small town experience of
                                solemn
        life, as could the clothes
a corpse waking wld surely wonder finding
In 15 minutes you
slept through
the nondescript
few organ pieces
   thought, Jesus
stuck here the night —
— I'd rather be
                dead!
dreamt I was the U.S. Bill of
Rights, people leaning over me
whose 20th generation badbreaths
fogged the bay window up above
in fern arrangements/in a room/
 full of strangers: without street clothes
no busfare — — Hell — I had at least two dollars
in change
on me when that bus hit me:
   then I began to smell the
   lilies, coming to life, knee deep in enemies . . .
in fern arrangements/in a room/
full of strangers
O death most cruel
   are thy pyjamas!

Folk Poem

My cats have ruined my life
It's as simple as that
Don't ask me to explain it
You might go and ask them
If they won't tell you anything why should I
They know damn well in spite of they ain't
                                    saying nothing
That silence don't fool me a bit I know
They have ruined my life they know
they have ruined my life   and I know
                              that they know
Don't think you've heard the last of me
                              on this matter.

Ishmael (you clever little fellow)
you really know how to frighten a guy
you fix on me with one eye
with the other
stare inward till your scalp
soaks your brain's scarlet up.

have your youth
have your little joke
but get older quickly
            and join us
  I'm frightened just thinking
at anything naive as you
If you suddenly saw
    the president of the United
    States coming at you with a hatchet
you'd yet find it in your child's heart
                    to forgive him .

mike —
   while I was waiting for you to come
   I browsed around some
   you were late coming
   so I stole a few stamps
     to use at home . . .
   no one's perfect.

   well here I was, a pocket full of
   stamps; it, half past
   the hour
   so I thought . . .
   my . . . you've had that bicycle
     up there for two years
   and never used it once; no one's perfect
   so I stole *it* too)
well —
   while I waited
     (for you)
    I also stole
   some dexedrine I'd
   found while I was
   looking through your drawers (which incidentally
   I stole also (not the dexedrine —
   the drawers
because —
   no one's perfect I'm
   leaving you this note (
so you'll know
   who was visiting
while I waited for you.
   you were two hours late
   so I left with everything —

   everything I could get my hands on that is (
   no one's
   perfect).

A Horrible Oath

I hope
the guy
that stole
my *Snatch No. 2*
comicbook from the
preserve of my study closet
just the other day
has met with
a fatal
erection — (1,
just too terrible,
fatal erection.)

must
have been
a friend / inside-job
/th freaky little shit — he'll
pass normally by but suddenly flash
hidden guilt — (he'll ask me
if I'm o.k. and I'll say: naw, course-not,
some motherfucker gonn'n ripp't off my R. Crumb/*Snatch No. 2* —
how would YOU/FEEL if THAT/HAPPENED to YOU, FRIEND, eh?
— He'll say something clever, like: zat-so-, huh, zatta-fact-all-right?)

,
me,
chiming/
in with a yessir,
thats-a-fact, its-so-all-righty,
and: — I know just WHO TH PISS-HEAD IS, cuz
THE MEMORY OF THAT LITTLE BOOK —
just DOESN'T WANNA QUIT,
and say, friend
wld-you-mind
not-pointing
that thing
towards
me?

Yes,

I'll eat ALL your mushrooms
You'll have to hide inside an orange
I'll pour thumbtacks in your boots
then dump molasses out
on the sidewalk —
so you'll NEVER get home,
yes, my dear,
when I'm THROUGH with you
they'll KNOW you were done.

Crude Robert

we talked about Robert
(her son) — I defended him,
then she'd defend him back —
then we fell
  to taking turns
  defending Robert .

(for hours   our asses
    glued to   naugahyde
       barstool covering

      we sat, sweated
&   defended Robert —
could've been any Robert.)

I am a surfer at 12 o'clock high
keeping to the crests of life
the good times will never pass me by

for I also have a large net I cast
out over the calendar
and it nets me some fine days

I dance free of the fates
like in a western where the cowboy
dodges every bullet

as approaching the prime target
or the gold mine
with bandits all around it

and suddenly one day I'll reach in
grab that bag of loot
and ride off on my horse.

you have never seen a man fuck a chicken
til you have seen the current pope of rome
                              fuck a chicken.
now there is a guy
who knows what chicken-fucking's all about.
one rainy easter,
I happened to catch his act.

well there stood Giovannee
beatific in his robes
grasping
this chicken
by its giblets
and boy oh boy did that frier
drop a feather or two.
Giovannee fuckt it til the bird could no longer cluck
til nothing clickt
til giblet gravy
made the pope's
glasses fog.

and that chicken tried so hard to please the pope
that when it died it went to heaven and still had its
                              wishbone intact;
so don't let them tell you
you can't take it with you
for when this bird saw god
it weren't squinting from no bucket.

Chicken Poem No. 2

when Rosalita put the poodle's
towards her stomach, insideways/out
she was (*un*abracadabra)/merely
genuflecting another crown-prince, unfrogg'd;
(which: was a fairy-tail/huzzahed the
audience / who, demanded to   see the ticket-
wicket-señor   about   THIS('s
really getting / perverted as
hell — we paid / hundreds of pesos to
see that mexican broad swallow a poodle '3 ways'
and you guys show us something even our wives
back home have no qualms about doing; NOW . . .
bring out a
        donkey
           and a
              . . . a . . .
— parakeet!

please shave my head
for a minute, for a joke
let me stand before
the door of a friend
and as he awkwardly invites me in
mutter Hare Krishna
and then I'd like my hair back again.

Five for Bruce

'became king
            of all of Scotland' and then
Robert Bruce
            you went on to die!

If there was no further humility
you would be made to suffer
as a label on a swim suit bought into Tangier
and fetched to Canada
                        by a Jew
it serves you right Robert
consorting with spiders
that are not even insects.

Robert Bruce 'Seafarer'
                        swim-where
where will you go   cold
                              dead
            and embarrassed?

But there is no lesson to be learned
from one who's dead and had
learned his own
from spiders

eight times
the damned thing crawled up th wall
like eight revolutions
of a South American country
and eight times
was it deposed; history
is desperate
has no choice
but to go ahead
for
      it, not even like an insect
is never finally ineffectual; it is not
written or recorded that way.

*

Then Ali·
          uncle to the prophet
swept thru Spanish history
with an Islam pushbroom
                    and when he'd finished
he was dead

          he'd found
-ed Tangier
          where I found my bathing suit
in the Thieve's Market there.

Robert Bruce was an arrogant
                              Scottish
thief, himself

          (history doesn't tell us this, tho)

They made him a noble chief
                          to rule
other thieves
            and thus
history is a local affair/written
as subjectively
            as one might apply
cosmetics to a dead corpse
thus being kind
to one's own future.

To talk of population however
would be to digress   from death
and the individual.

          Robert Bruce
stumbled down Sir Walter Scott's Scotland
down little paths that wound
round brooks and lakes
where crude the monster

that made all Scots
frugal, frugally, himself,
dwelt in a submarine cave
'prehistorically.'

*

From South America
            the urgent message comes
        : Send tractors,
                    and more guns —
    as many guns as you can!)

While I am neatly folding
your tattered bathing suit
into a parcel to be sent
home to Canada where it never belonged

                    Robert Bruce,
you've been defiled so many times
another time wouldn't matter — besides
I read somewhere that you had patience
which virtue
            you'd either stolen
or saved, tho, tattered,
                    like any good Scot
from an ancestry of your clan.

The Scottish were not Seafarers, the English
have had a great joke
                    sending your name
to Tangier
            on a cloth postcard

    eight times that
    same spider   or
        was it seven times
        that he climbed up that wall?
History
        is not unkind to you, Robert Bruce,

it allowed you to travel
       and be different images.
Things are defiled
              according to their own attitudes
during life and after
                the dead
themselves being not
              particular
 -ly holy.

And that is how you spread to Canada
and parts of South America.

                         *

'Come into my
parlour said the
Spider to the fly'

                    (after his narrow escape
from the prison cell
              where both he and Robert Bruce
were sharing scraps of metaphysical gossip.

Come into my life more fully
said I
       to history, let me see
a maximum
              of transportation and free
associations —   but let nothing
bind people
to spiders.

Let me swim with your nonsense
written inches above the crack
my ass becomes as it rounds out
toward the top of this
metaphysical
swim-suit.

I'll send you back to Scotland someday
                                        I promise
you'll see Scotland
as prophetic Moses did
looking thru a small bird's eyes

                              if you could cross the Atlantic
seven more times
                try to rest at ease in the Hills
of your native countree-o

Tho History might make me
a liar in this life time
and your soul will see no rest
in images
            spread thin as mustard
on a New York dog

But spiders always are being born
in the form of capability
                      or illusion
and you can travel
                  out of prison
in any manner of disguises
in any life form or time.

                    *

Or is an image
sacrilege
in that it never dies
and my promises
are short-sold by History?

To you Robert Bruce
there will be
            no peace, no
historic truce
for one who shares
his wisdom with a spider.

                    The famous
are only unusual/they did nothing
that could in fact be called   'great' — Marat
has only survived
all of these years
because of a skin ailment
or whatever he did
in his sewer bath tub.

A poem about you Bruce
was written
                by a singular Jew
whom history
                may choose to
totally disregard in that

he too stood
                on top of the Empire State Building
much as Henry Miller did
and
     he too saw little crawling things
and saw them scheming to get out/only
it was with the greatest reluctance
he rode down some eighty stories
to join them again.

MIXED DOUBLES

(with Geoff Young)

for David Smith

ONE

My year 4: moving forms, ice cream flower odors, fears
Sleeping in sunlight
It's the ocean of western steel
Indeed, the nerves take up the chase
The wings of a dog
Which has a live bird in its mouth
Buildings embankment parkway grass and river
Each of us must pay for a woman
But, no no, I want a cure!
The dead are no good: dead or alive — they stink!
I wet my finger and put it to the wind
All evaporated, nobody real
Suddenly I see with such clear eyes
The hilt of the swords! the hilt of the swords!
Thus all roads are perfectly safe
                              and at any hour
To rest in their eyes we learn movement
Skip the rumble, move into the inference
Sitting up in the chair, a bed only big enough for one

TWO

5: praise from a grandmother for a mud pie lion
You occupy me so completely
Bugles that make me want to listen
Tongue crushed by the weight of its flavors
And the taste of the-to your eyes-invisible crystals irradiates
    the world
Crowns what you are doing in the present deed
Whose sweetheart will plant flowers in your helmet?
A little chocolate tomb for a dead maraschino cherry
It's a matter of being handled
Of happiness not reached and reached
Whose strangeness crushes in the only possible embrace
Sinking in velvet pity and self-hate
What does one do with all this crap?
My o'ertaxed brain, in its units, hangs on between
Bright cornices of eavesdropping palaces
And it is such a private thing the thing they do

THREE

6: the found book of nude marble women hidden by a
School-teaching methodist mother
Runs through my brain as warm
To the parting of the trees
The right kind of accident begun
My images stalk the trees and the slant sap's tunnel
While the veins sow red pearls of evil
The mute intention we call love
Klong of gong hit with sock full of sand
A couple of specifically anguished days
Where the seven spades dig a moat around you
Massive pretenses to anxiety, the animal's dream
Scribbling, swearing between his teeth
Each man wants the pomegranate for himself
Are we just muddy instants?
Alone, between obscure signs
Whizzed the Limited — roared by and left

FOUR

Diana of the Ephesians
Chemicals and melted gold
I have watched your shadow go by
Like intemperate smiles, in a
Hieroglyphic table of human passions
The body nothing more than a bag of earth
On the buffalo skin of the prairies

The placid glimmering of distant stars,
The tape of my mother does not have that high pitch
Picking fruit in one dream & storing it in another
If this is what life is,
Could one of your Gods not do it better?

At the irregular stones, iridescent sandgrains,
Her red lips of Hollywood, soft as a Titian and as tender
This is the point of likening, this is the world
If we can get by that whiskered bird
She remembers. She puts it all together.
Rise shining martyrs, out of the movie house's matinee

FIVE

Egyptian embalmers and the sepulchral barge
Spread out wings to the ends of my fingers
Storm coat evangelistically ground —
How difficult it is to dissolve!
A horrible lucidity, defines us what we are
So much wing, so much farewell, so much love
That things flock up in the face of the sun
Elastic flexible yes but this is awful
My brain! a living thing
Now radio voices cry population hunger world
The silence that lasted for a quarter of a century. All
Outcry of discovery, sensation or pain;
I knew the actual ache of my arms reaching
There where I was splattered, now taken in its guise

SIX

The fight between the monster Tiamat personification of
Chaos darkness disorder evil and Marduk god of light
Reaches my heart and stops
Our of spun glass and silver threads
Comedy drips on the grass stages
The indomitable Yankee cactus;
For me there is no getting off
And I by this will be a gainer too
Less the illuminating analysis of a conjunction
But don't make your clean body too visible
Dawn must always recur
To blot out the stars and the terrible systems of belief
None wide enough to hold you in
I emulate the black which is a cry but is not voluptuary
        like a warning
And in the mean time my songs will travel
The last of knowing is the first of innocence
Through the fireplaces spurting through the chimneys

SEVEN

Where water is the parent of all things — where universal
Darkness reigns — where gods have been forgotten
My face will be buried in ice. Luxuriant anxieties!
When stars are in my head, and we
Get into the birdcage without starting them singing
Remember always the barriers so cupiditously defended
They have their exits and their entrances
If I open my eyes it's not to see you
Oh shadow of the silence's deep echoes
This is the other canyon
Our minds have suffered from bees
Our junk lives of cell destruction; discard yr universe
Lose your marbles making it
Like so many squids, for sweetness. Do you have the haveness
Of those who love or know or notice us, those
Resolving the enigma of the fever chart
What actual gardener turning the dark earth
Or some poor stranger who comes by

EIGHT

Face illuminated by the sun and moon
If a bird what kinds
Are apart and together, friend of my youth
You will go higher than the steps
I will watch here for the movement
A pillar in duplicate, a pillar
The kinship of woe and mortality, we know,
Too splendid and precise in its assembly

Cell by cell the baby made herself, the cells
Made cells
Baby with my name, old five weeks
Are your hands big enough to cover your face?
Like a painting by Picasso! You fled when you followed
The wealthy curled darlings of our nation
When I was still a willing wife
Clear and careful, knowing always the exact peril

NINE

The Babylonian hero wrestling the lion
Nothing I have ever seen in air
Whom I've so recently met — a fragment of the universe
Wears a short red-plaited skirt & a dark blue jersey
Weeping for his own ugliness
And beneath their shivering dance the houses
Pious. Adorn Her feet with flowers, perfume, gaudy ribbon-bows
Letters that arrive moist, messages I translate;
Every bone in me belongs to others
Organized, as perfect as an army there
Salvation babies, saved people, Messiah's men, not
Taken with a slight spitting motion from between teeth and
        whanged into place
Though the observers appear clear
You are lean, achieved, ravished, acute, light, tan
Game unmentioned when we met, roar
Mouths biting empty air
Changing phrase within the phrase
As gently it starts to deepen and slowly increase

TEN

tossing a bull
you fly through earth and water
in our coats, a believable doubling
seeking personal chemical fortune
we strip off our pretty blazers
nostrils of pain down avenues
again we dismantle the motorcycle
and grope beneath the most serious labor
each time my heart is broken it makes me feel more adventurous
pieces of the past arising out of the rubble
and a climax means a splash in the pool
alien and healthy, for death is here and knowable

come in, fare well in me
on the beach fraught with emotion and rotting elephants
I think of talking and man
the folding and lapping brightness
the rattling marbles of granulation. vivo! the dextrose
twin alloy to true counsel
by evening light, at the window, where wind blows

ELEVEN

Standing on a gryphon
Casting a red shadow
Of the fresh currents of doubt and
A prehistoric sloth nails me to this moment
I cast deep, angry looks at the moon
Do I have to gather more mothers?
Love and hate go back where you came from
I am tired of purposes
A few inches of adhesive tape seals the mouth
The cat is cleaner when he licks
The imperceptible moan of covered breathing
Balustrade, tensile, enclosing the surging waters of my heart
The night's end foreknown, furred roommate
I can't stop thinking about those who really knew
Like an unbelievable story escaping the believing mind, a
Singing in my fingers at the textures
That young men hope for. Aimlessly

TWELVE

The carrying of mud bricks by yoke and cord
The door wakes me
Thought! a winter climate
Hence, I am your pupil, the neck
wrenched with pride
stomach, the brute beast emerges and stands
on the timid globe of an orange
one-armed, one-legged, and one-headed,
and I am forced to write "belly" when I mean "love"
measured to smoothness and perfect in line.
Send me the norths of language
as in a rainbow the end keeps leaping toward the middle
But for something to read in normal circumstances?
Pleasures to enter the dream, to enter together we said
and hold your hollow breath there in the dark.
Therefore, this afternoon, as never before, I walk

THIRTEEN

the dialectic of survival
this is your jewelled reptilian eye
found in the Southern Hemisphere and where
tricked out in tartan stripes for a harlequinade
babies cannot manage crocodiles

I love to watch children dying.

All at once I go to the window. It is a square
A two-legged dog hunting a new horizon of howls.
But sometimes I gather evidence of a kind
to cry and laugh at the same time
But the torment of others remains an experience
similar to the sole support of a love affair, so artful,
this whippet sense, a sulk

wise, but so unloosed as hamstrung.
Here I sit resisting their rich meat.
We have kept our erasers in order.

FOURTEEN

Everything I sought, seek
In darkness next to mine —
I am who offers you to wear,
If only for its being graceful,
The water and the customs and the white mud;
Weave the print of rude crude words.
Rise, snap down and rise dreaming

Except a pause for breath on the peak
The reward is to be a source
In dry half-dreaming supplication . . .
Or the ground this house is on,
The far field, the windy cliffs of forever

What the work really is in relationship with birds and insects
I regret very much to inform you.
We build upon a field of lies
Truths of the imagination
No matter how lost, twisted and illegible
You give me screaming fits of sheer adulation

FIFTEEN

What I will die not finding
(When a hole is filled, where does it go?)
Shining feathers of hair sift over my forehead
And in this storm, along the tooth of the street
Shards of instinct, nonetheless, compel me
And today is not worth haggling over
And today is not worth haggling over

I know there is someone composed of my pieces
Insanity in high places
Proceeds in brittle nightgowns
As squirrels inhabit a geometry
I would be of their number & of their dumbness

Of heldness and of caresses you have become the entrepreneur
But genius is an enormous littleness, a trickling
It is the definition of the rope that ought to interest
An electric system
I stop in my room toward the East, quiet, quiet

5 JOCKEYPOEMS

                              I felt
                            that if
                           all
                                my
                     poems
                were   in   the
                                shape
              of a jockey   riding a
                                horse
        there would   be a
damn
      good chance
              noone   would
                                    ever
        notice
            their   prose
          fab-
        ric

feb 21/22 77

```
                        another
                               day
                   another poem
                          in the
                                    shape
                 of a jockey riding his horse
            often I worry that if the last poem
            I wrote shaped thus is somewhat different
          in size than this one is, well ...   that the series
        all I'm trying to do
            the whole thing              would  fail
                                             hands
                                    on the  reins
            ass  jacked
            up
               in the air            knees doubled
                                             under
                                    my  jockey
                                  and why should I worry?
              but I do. It's
                        the feet
                   my man has dug
                        into
                        his horse's flanks:   what if
          the horse
                   doesn't
                        like it?
```


feb 21/22, 77
   2nd jockeypoem

good ?
             your poems   not
      why are   because
      they don't rhyme but because each
      is the shape, the perfect shape
      of a jockey
                    riding
                         his
                         horse.

      the horse sits underneath
                    the jockey's
                         heels
                    dig into that
                         horse's hide
            and horses have soft skin
            if not a trifle discoloured
                 now your man
                 is standing
                 on a wooden
                 horse/how
                 sad/how/
                 going nowhere!

3rd jockeypoem
2.22.77

sometimes I aim to get   the air around the jockey
leaving   the   jockey   his horse   alone; the air
around the jockey
the arch of his back   the air
                               in front of
                               his face

the air he will breathe
                                   next
and I think

this what they   found   when after
the radiation   danger   was over
they strolled
the streets of
Hiroshima: jockeys   pumping hell out of
horses who couldn't
                get out.   in pompeii
      there is a statue   of a boy
and that boy is running
or rather, the statue of that boy
is running, and under that boy's
                     arm
              is a   loaf of thousand year old
         bread and   you know
        there's a fly   on that loaf, that
   thousand year old loaf; a thousand year old fly!

4th jockeypoem   22.2.77

the ; the
the ---'s

if you hold the baby up to her mother
she will accept or she will reject that baby
if you hold the poem shaped like what was hewn away from another poem
whose silence
was that other's noise
            what will you get but the mountain
                before the invention of carved jade
                    a carving of the eclipsed sun
against a background of dark day, the bright ring, the darkness registering twice
            what I carved had not been seen til I freed it from its rock
            the robes fell to the floor like so many chips of monarchy
            like Versailles under the wreckingball.

5th jockeypoem 2.22.77

SOME OF THE CAT POEMS

for. . . .
        (among the living) Squamuglia, Manfredonia, Felix. .
and. . .Pulsifer, Rork, Ghostie, Teddy, Fluff. . . . .

I was rather surprised to learn that A. Gold was putting together a book of cat poems. For years he has fought it out with his cats. It would seem they have won ... Mr. Gold, not to slander but rather lay the facts straight, has an allergy to cats. Furthermore, he talks disrespectfully to them, thinking they don't understand what he is saying. It peeves me so much to think of this I can hardly go on with my task. Obviously, cats are close to me. To talk about them ... I ... I go all giddy, roll on my back and begin to purr. I cannot understand the strange distance A. Gold is apart from his cats that allows him to sit back on his typewriter and coolly every few months knock out a poem about them. I shake my head. He sneezes.

— *The shortstop of the heart.*
Dec. 1977

The rain has stopped
but left everything so sad
wet and sad. I offer my hand

into the sky. past the
roof of the tent my jacket makes
it tastes no dryness yet. The sky

recalls in its strange manner
demands what has fallen
back from the grass. I pass

a wet red fire
hydrant glistening the rain
has made it fantastically rich

and along the concrete ditch
an orange cat rushes
its coat dry.

Looking up the source the sky
is beautiful mysterious
with clouds moving quickly disbanding.

april 68, mtl

I confess
I cannot
put broken cats
back together but neither
can god) .

in his effort
to be free
or seem so
our big grey
ran miles away

you could have seen his silhouette
leaping like a made up mind
across balconies
below streetlight moons

that old streak of stubbornness
taken to drinking from other
toilets or overturned
garbage pail covers

where rain gathers downwards
in abnormal sonatas.

How the death of a cat
whose remains I haven't found
is hardly acceptable

though th cat is so much deader
whose remains
are never found.

                 as things die finally (and
                 only once they have left us
through a wooden door
or everyday conception.

          I shout
                 from the back porch
                 like Stanley Spencer
          hopelessly writing to his wife
          for any assurance her grave held
that the dead
are truly dead
and now
          can be ignored

     but cats are never famous
and only can contrive
to love us as a wife might.

                 dead things
                      move forever
                           through the night

     backwards ,
     through the head.

Three days
old fat
pussycat
that you've been away
but still there
can be no celebration
               till the body has been found.

I should not be awake. I glance out in to
the night. why there is my lovely tomcat.
I have a feeling I should not be here.
The stillness unwinds ticking like
a home movie projector whirrrrr .
brrrrr I'm plunged out with him
into the night's cold air and I
hang like drapes gathered twice
I forget to breathe leaning now
farther out my bedroom windowsill
the night's black silence the air's
mysterious chill takes away my
breath tugging me into this
tapestry of stealth I pour out of
my window's high rectangle
a little like the mind that has
just mastered some difficult
algebraic equation.I and cat.

My cat wrapped in a box
carling's red cap ale
sleeping small

I smoke my pallmalls
the package that   says
I'm particular

the house disarray — we're moving
Our wooden lion
staring at a crate

vases on a shelf
touching like
they never were before

there's restlessness
in the little space
my typewriter's set up in.

I feel the need
to ponder
the habits of the last year

the cat still sleeps in his box
I relax
we'll move him just as he is.

A sketch of a cat . the cat
since disappeared . the lapse of time;
dead I must admit / after one year.
the sketch has not changed. no attempt
to free itself , merge with the disappearance.

    An address too, still on the once clean sheet
less urgent now in its removal. Willard-
it must be his address/ he too,
long gone /that too,
several winters ago;
a double spring
has erased
every presence
but the yellow sheet of paper;
scotch taped edges.

kittylitter and something else I remembered yesterday
you left me left not a trace of either
though I'm now not sure what it was I needed then

need has such scope, travelling in quantum
    that I have no fear however
of not needing ever again what you didn't
leave me any of

next time you go let's talk first.
I am your collaborator in this
life; even if they aren't your bloody cats or my
    bloody cats. they make us second cousins

    I had hoped last   time you went away what you didn't say
    wouldn't happen this time you went away but it did didn't it
    this note is retroactive
        as is my anger.

I leave this folded like a suit
for you to come across in my closet

I would never frighten you by leaving a suit in my closet:you,
my collaborator!

Our big grey cat fat
head proverbially
                    quizzical
lying prone   eyes dumb

to us perhaps a nap
of innocence
                    satisfactory
that fat old cat's life.

again moving; snuggling
toward these sun
                    rays
creating a spot
dropping lazily

frequently a misplaced
guitar note
                    demanding
better comprehension always
resting after completely

satisfied with some explanation
available to cats.

chased by a lion up the spiral of my body
I roll home. what schemes inhabit a citizen
band radio on your wide wrist. O sadness
is knowing your phone number !
You are all the long nights and the empty
cottage cheeses. The pale yellow amethysts
the tumbler lying on its side on the darkened rug
you are an ever widening stain
you are something that can't be contained
you are communism you are the fire before
the firemarshalls. you are my cat in the tallest tree
so high up / it is hopeless
you are me turning my back on my cat
walking away with my shoulders slumped
you are the effect of the light upon my shadow as
it drapes upon the lawn
the wistful gaze of a neighbor as slowly
he
slides down a window and wanders over
to the television set. You are a long
night. I will get used to you I guess.

Cat gazing at what
first was a buzzing, then
realized to be
to me, at any rate, a fly.

imperceptible squealings
impossible postures rising
sheer intent alone could kill that fly
if that's how flies were meant to die.

the light reflected off
a pane of brilliant glass
no doubt focuses itself

immediately below, a cat
its four legs moving like
a barber's two pairs
of scissors
cuts across a lawn
slanted obliquely
towards a sidewalk
on whose lap
falls
the marigolds

the brown velvet of the cat
the thing it strides towards
the green against
which it strides, releasing
that green

above the house
the blue
above & beside
the pinprick of a
chimney.

no doubt focuses itself.

july 1/76

The black cat anoints the grey
with a blow withheld
the two by their dinner dishes
the grey looking demure as hell
finally draws off slithering down the hall
as the black cat turns back craning his head
to see what he won.

my cat has kind of a mange of the ass
sleeps as though its mind was a blown tube
all day long its uninteresting life passes by it instead of it by
it watches daytime television, indoor things are slow
if I blew a loud whistle against its ear it would be fearful for a week
but then settle down again as if to say to sudden things, hah! , a week late
ahh, a nosespray junkie, overweight and underworried somehow its dreams
tune in on the dustmotes that travel across the kitchen on a sunbeam
I am high in the alps kissing the tits of a sunny cow breeze against my fur;
I have just won a quiz show and everything is going with me to Hawaii for 5 mths.
You should have seen me before the family moved; then I knew worried, not now.

feb 4, 77

puddy/
comes in
I patch his ear
he's off again/
pit-stop!

hearts in their mouths discovered
they beat like small pianofortes
they scram to the ground headless

and heedless of their small
breakable limbs: for this is death
the large claw extends up to

the highest bough climbable:it
is where they steal from, they load
six cherries not white absolutely

three in each small pocket and they
begin the descent all wrong:like
a cat gone too hastily up the pole

of a telegraph, they run away from
the hand that threatens, by running
first towards it: backwards like a cat

but they will not leap at the eyes
of that voice, they stand there
sensing a human punishment finally.

june 17.77

11 years — Candy says that's
53 cat years. I don't rightly like to say
anything. Try to think of some reason

that cat should go on living.
accepts his old age as a handicap —
seems cats live till they die.

The snow is too deep & has gone on for too many days.
It's ruined my whole winter and has turned my cats rest-
less & against me. they drape their bodies over riblike
coils of radiators almost grilling, 3 cats 5 radiators;
a park-full of area; complete attendance; total silence
three meows sounding like eachother, like the word: sum-
mer in by landslide/ if cats had the vote. separately
now, meow around the room, each waits for cue twice a-
round then gordon, who might have kittens anyday, was
too eager. I am in the middle victimized by this kanga-
roo court meowing in turn each meow pops off like a
flashcube like photos framed on dressers; 3: asking the
question/ do I love this person..? 6 eyes plant discon-
tent. DO YOU UNDERSTAND- I can't make it spring before
it will be due- this one, I. puzzle over. /do their
eyes drill me less or differently? no; what can I do for
them: make winter shorter? raise their IQ's for my de-
fense I am not guilty /then lower them, 100, 80, 60, 30, 15,
14,13, 12/ first meow, next at intervals of each 1 point,
would it matter if the brightest was dumbest. they want
to say We trust you over & over again like waifs in war-
time poland. they also mean with the same plea that trust
grows tense imperfect. They'll settle for nothing less
than something new on their minds, these 3 today they're 3
bitchy gargoyles, coldstony, decked in sable useless 3
waitresses who come to your table at the same time each
claim to you a lie, each wants to move to someplace bet-
ter make more easier money. they didn't think like that
at all yesterday and it will be gone before lunchtime
tips are missed. but these cats don't know ups and downs
total-up they get so happy they ricochet off walls like
tree-jaguars hunting and my signed Tiffany in ten thous-
and pieces of gold-pink glitter and now this is too sad
they indeed suffer it's what cat's aren't made for.

I'll give you summer I'll give you summer I mumble, one
eye arches, closes. I feel they mean to make me keep this
promise. You can't talk to cats, they follow me about
the rest of the day, looking everywhere, back to me,
even scratch to open the hall closet door.

They peer for summer like it were a bone and buried,
or another person, who could do better for them. I am
the key, the guy to see In & out they go in between pos-
ing like alarmclocks who might practical joke get me
off the hook! Persephone pack yer weekend-bag hop a
plane & present yerself at my doorbell; Be the first to
ring & be calling on these furs. feed them one slice
even a platecrumb of summer afternoon. Don't apologize!
sometimes they stay out longer than other times, my day
ruined by winter, I sit and let'em in & out as patiently
as an old man in an elevator; only when they don't prac-
tically/ bounce, back; I figure I know exactly why. sigh-
ing. they look up old cat acquaintances of late fall
days, follow them home, dive into a neighbor's, to get-
bootedout as/ 1-cat-too-many, march home wondering looking
from side to side and outwards, if the outside of each
house, has fallen victim to the same winter scene,
sometimes they drag their minds and bodies and voices all
at once, weave down the long hall, broken-hearted. like
I once did when I'd not been able to reach my muse, day
after day, I collected bluer sombrer feeling jilted be-
ginning to feel the cartoon of misery, museless useless
then came the poem as I conceded on time, though late as
always. the hole was too deep to smile & shrug, the poem
waited for my typed initials, those cats will just have
to tread water till spring till the snow too has fully
bowed before the idea of so early a spring. cats first
winter.

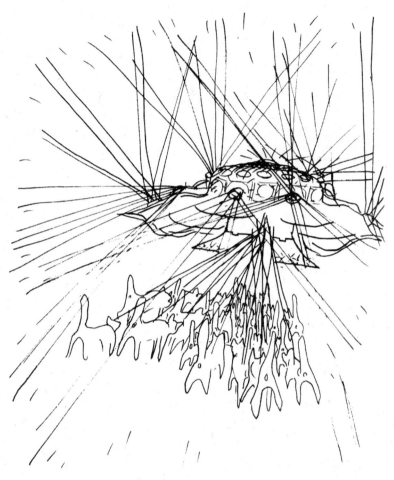

close encounters of the cat kind.

BEFORE ROMANTIC WORDS

Chrysler would come into the gallery, ask Joseph Hartert the price of a painting and proceed to bargain. By Stansky's account, Hartert might say, "it's $150."

"Hmmm," Chrysler might reply. "$150. Are you sure it's $150, Joe?"

"Yes, $150."

"You know that's a Picasso, don't you, Joe? You're sure you want $150?"

"If you say it's a Picasso, it's your business. The price is still $150."

Sonnet

There is something crapulous and far from the sawdust
sticking my head into this large mouseholed garland
outside tamer than a dram of scotch in the yearly ocean of suburbia
the noise of a passing perambulator's squeak is all I get
I fired on the fourheaded asshole concern I remember in a poem
that would reach their friends and make them my enemies
and nothing throughout the course of this act raised itself to the level
of even mild drama; I walked vaguely uncomfortably away thinking, shit,
why didn't I fart during the silence instead of yelling halfwaythrough
the second act; their audience may have resented the incursion on their
                                                    sabbatical from culture
and this soon ceased to bother me and they soon ceased for me to exist.
the reality less than a dream doesn't stand up to the sun of 11 a.m.
what is it to do when noon looks down its collar and poleaxes it ?

Shut in by this rain pedalling incessant as a bicycler
glued to the thought of summer because it is August
and not fully willing to survive this holocaust

I shove aside all the mail I had been waiting weeks for
like a hungry man who'd pounded the table, his plate,
and play with my typewriter, my knife and fork

in this life there is the villainy of *upset.* I know it
with the time of my life *unread.* my friends kicked
aside is where my kingdom my habits are

poor company, mildewy intentions I am not one to get
involved with. backstage I am at your door; a
bouquet of poison sumac, *pounding!*

Strange to compare the laundromat
lit at night, with my heart. The lights
jarr, as in any analogy there are
elements that mean something because
they must ; but mean nothing
                              because they cannot.
So the lights on in my heart
that are not lights, that is not
a laundromat, are strange to me. Mis-
placed, somewhere in a corner outside
the path traversed, the understanding ground
I stand, or am, locked
                        or perhaps not,
the laundromat I pass though late at night
needn't be, who thinks of trying the door
it is the light alone that is foreboding
enough in itself; keeps customers away.
And in my heart, also tumblers, secret
safe, silent. distant lonely unlit
                              a night
passes, but has just begun.

Glue your genitals
   to a pasteboard
        kimono
   and you are
   no longer
        mysterious
   to your Self.

The mirror knows
     or seems to.
Perhaps the man inside
isn't looking exactly at us.
Perhaps the confrontation is what
is exact about the excitement. I know
that if I was being watched by someone as
excited as I was, there I'd stand behind my own
pasteboard excitement
     laid emotional stark bare
       as a line of french chalk across the grey hem
  of flannel trousers
       I would think, you marked this
     because you wanted this
     and feel the soft flannel
giving way as the scissors
            worn to a frazzle by
   the headcold of impossible assent
 close the eyes and allow the steel to chew through the hem
 munching like gum.
That second the eyes don't see.
It is impossible to give assent
the self is caught in the zipper
of crazy erotic stammering
and chewn to pieces.
    the pasteboard gives up
    the tailor no longer
  holds the fabric to the self
 (who no longer holds against
the world/
that cutting.

sex at thirty-one
a golden shower for the milkman
the sun setting on a lake
regret

the phone rings
hesitation
is it the girl who . . ?
onyx

her name was Amanda
she trains her cool breath to travel the length of your body
 outside a police whistle blows
you think: children . .
rolling over

we are caught in the rain
running, running, newspapers over our heads
Amanda shrieks
you don't turn around because of the newspaper over your head
no leopards

I trace five red dots on your upper inner thigh
and think: constellations
still they are not all home

the whistle has gone
it has begun to rain
the same shriek or you are not sure

something you possibly wanted to do
I am thirty-one today, only that was yesterday.

begin rolling windows up
the picnic blanket
the trunk
where are the lids ? the lids to everything…

and you look up and there
is a rainbow
the most beautiful rainbow
you ever have seen.

youth I did a rope trick
which dirty mistake burnt it

at the speed of a lost
captive balloon my eyes
climb into the cloudy space
                    of overhead

like when a badger burrowing
overly deep's
heart is struck by panic just as
his talons break through
                    to hell

going up I came upon a solid wall

sex at thirty-one

Is like love at seventeen. it plies deep
Affords the illusion there is nothing else.

Every few years kicks sand in the face of everyfew years
Love, only a pornography of the heart has a habit of being

Waylaid, it had a habit of suddenly throwing down
Its basket of roses and running. rape, basic call of thing

Changed, suddenly and love dies like drool on a napkinless chin
Love gives way to one of love's perversions. dry skin

To wetness. even the idea of sex glistens. like the heart
Thinking of where it left its bubblegum. the heart

Is a dry old taskmaster. its puppies are like the grains
of sand dragged on to a picnic blanket. as the afternoon

Turns into death. count love with a slight chill. too many
Times love has occurred, reared its beautiful head. we are sick

Sick of change. sick of wind change. sick of lifeguard change
Sick of the tides of the heart.

Here 400 miles off Wall Street
Fitted with various hardware —
It is understood I'm bought & paid for; I,
Knowing this , accepted this , knowing well
My rights vanish with this purchase.

Please, try to not pat me each
time I pass your admiring form —
It is enough that I'm totally yours.
Allow me freedom to a point, perhaps
my mind tests the tether of my leash

But I would be back automatically
at most I might resist you
through several mealtimes
But back automatically would I insinuate
myself under your roof; your need for
worry , lessened; my reasons same as before.

again & again will I puzzle away
at your control of me ; its absence,
tightened by my absence; we will
one by one move down testing links
of some finite chain that may yet
resist my trial tugs, until & also, pulled taut/

I am bought ; I am yours .
when I balk you inherit
the tuggings of my constant dissatisfaction
a transaction /I trust because you do,

you pull me as I pull you as in fairness
I utilize all loopholes you've left me free of
just as you are free to tax these rash-escapades.

the things I want to continue
the things
I wanted
to continue / there are so many reasons
to stop life

yet I don't know quite that that is what I want
the not wanting
it is not what I want

I have an inability to assimilate
life's curves
I am over the Atlantic
 with clouds
it is a globe's sky
 I arch around
 with the lines
I am going to Europe
 like a dream (life is)
in which I always
    am setting out for Europe
and then the clouds
and then the cold
the north moves in
and I'm off course
and though I'm still going to Europe
I'm not going TO Europe
 and I awake
 with that expressed inability
to accept
O I believe..
but TO ACCEPT..

Out here the sun is a boss's weapon
the weekend the tampon of the working man

weeping at the clock
he puts his back to the shovel

communism travels ahead of thought
it belongs like a voice owns its yodel

the east is the cradle of thought
it is where the sun doesn't set on this hell

a blue heron flies to the suburbs on pay later
even symbolism is bottlenecked

we may have freedom
but it cannot be identified.

Draculae teeth swim in the fluid balance of my days
the ifs are so assorted the boxlid takes a bow before audience
who've yet to swing shut their earnest kimonos so drafty
in this argumental house yet no human has noticed: I am a pipe.

sphincters of salal donut the corridors of the year, pity
january is so proclaimed that we catch february unprepared, it
is the rodeo cowboy, it, the man goes down into the heart of august
he investigates why the charge went off twice; it goes off a 3rd time.

I am leaning on a rail wondering why I don't smoke, below activity
small as the tits on barbie dolls passes like leaves on a conifer. We
were about to be handed an important telegram but the day sighed
and changed its mind. I heard an attaché case snap succinctly shut...... .

In the soft plaid mesquite
she extends her arms to me. the sun

has set. it is cool. she rolls
her spine. languors. it is evening

the sun on one side the twinkle
as a planet leaves a hole in the sky

black pin-pointed small shadows
yet these things dazzle. my ease

to lie here never break the spell
linger ing until the dark

black shadows ease into total black
I ease into her arms and

all the black is western bright
all the evening mystic indian.

I wave my hand touch green; digest
the low blossom of the earth

and she is still
by my side. nightfall.

when I speak to you the cities cease to exist
there is only you
a pencil of doubt, no larger
than a tenement

the hesitancy in the space between my words
the times that wait for the times words
will be spoken, like clotheslines
fluttering
in the silence between

in the silence my words and your words
the winds of humanity rip an old towel to shreds
twisting it
it for a second looks to you like a codpiece
your finger goes to your lips

at some busy intersection of an invented city
a few cars squeeze by.

alison

I am alerting you to the fact that the clouds
above your house are doing a dance THIS MINUTE
and if I wait, well..

but I have already waited, a human faculty, thinking
what if the clouds by the time you have woken
have flown, disarranged themselves, gone to Europe

I juggled this thought unconscious of the lapse of time
while the clouds stayed and stayed. now the clouds can't say:
c'mon, Artie, wake her up. we are here only briefly

or Artie the day is glorious, take your time, ponder
this human condition you talk of. we are here
at your beck. we are like the photo of beautiful day

drawn from the textbook of surrealism, surrealism,
the everyday that never happens. and the clouds are gone.
a personal experience. which for you, never was.

so I leave a note on your doorstep; alison, wake up —
the clouds can be beautiful!

Chinese

I prayed you would be on time . .
then, I prayed you would be early
as the trombones slipped the day off the evening's wrists
and what the sunflowers stared at dissolved

a scent of pungent carrot filled the sudden and still air
and everywhere things slipped
back into the lake

night spread its ripple
catching me alone

you appeared like a bird
sweeping above my boat.

I will make a motion
for the pure lyric beauty of the wave,
the world
will never catch me with my pants down

I will design an America
of highways
and at its Kansas, slip in

inserting myself among all the traffic
insinuating I belong
drinking
tanksfull, for the pure lyric energy.

strange how in this world
each of us must somehow invent
I   have so scaled down love
when intending it for you
years might pass of you not
on the phone I couldn't care
the awesome thing love was
before reinventing personally
I didn't dare. -or you didn't
to be fair I all but swamped you
I redirected every discovery
you were all my intentions.

today

when no letters fall   like leaves
I am using the peace

I rake my sentiments (but not my friends) into
one neat pile
   I would like to get organized   but to me
   a union seems sinful and clerical
I want to walk around everywhere I go in far softer shoes
so my feet   fall like leaves   not like rain
   things pleased by my rewards
   mustn't feel bashed upon the head
by association I don't rule anything out but I doubt
whether you, cruelest month, time when everything is mailed to me
and suffocatingly heavy   will find a position at my table d'hôte
for which I'll be revenged I'm sure).

                           — *after Frank O'Hara)*

we know the weather of August
like a sentence to be primarily
about A.Gold not August just as
justice is about crime
not justice

behold these sleepy truths
like a victim on pentathol

who is created equal
-to the weather even ?

There is a space in my life
a woman could walk into
and fill / if she didn't jiggle
tremble / fidget / shake

When the sun is out and shadows
are long / you could drive
a truck through it. Women

walk around it; it scares 'em
this big, huge, gaping
hole in the middle of Artie Gold

They would rather
go to Texas
or get caught walking
in the rain

Well I have put my signs out
and I will just sit here
for a while
pretending my eyes are closed.

Drawn before me like swans
I sometimes think I have a hard-on I don't have
such is the force of life.

and is acted on and upon
to mysteriously over fifty years lose its potency
like some car battery

this is truly the desert.
I have an image of six motorcyclists making it hot for me
and when I lead them back

and jump into my car, it
like the hard-on of an old braggart queen, ceases
as chains strike the safetyglass.

no worry the sexual lamp of the days will turn down its tits
and my grumblings will be real like chestnuts
as if a yellow rain would make the sky green, no.

my professional opinions continue. a real poet/
a quacky human being. hah. aren't we all. some of us just not
failures at the top. the frontier varies with what it is seen
against. one foot in Switzerland, the bullets still pour over
my shoulders like sweat. unless you are standing on an alp you

cannot see I'm home free. in my trophy room , spending my money
which, is grumblings. it's the local currency.(I was Swiss..).

life.

                    In a sense
it is the exact opposite of what we want   and
that opposite isn't death
                    but fence.
somewhere over the rainbow
you see,   it's parabolic.
sometimes stretched out on drugs that make me taller
I sway over two kingdoms of sidewalk concrete   adjacent
but over the line. clothes vanish through the magic agency of drugs
naked to my brain my genitals hang like a child's drawing of scissors
open large enough only for the beam of life to shine through
I trap the living photon and aim it down. my friends say: Artie,
 you have dropped your handkerchief.

private   eye

only the hands of bugs bunny are deft
the two magpies have different colour beaks
they can be the three marx brothers
superman plays baseball with himself
ma & pa kent I suspect are redneck, vote
the wrong way on issues. want to repeal the tenth amendment.
gotham city is chicago not new york
metropolis might be baltimore, possibly atlanta
I have learned that ma & pa kent were clumsy axemurderers,
snooping, I have found things out that make me want to
                                            throw up.
professor Lang does not go to egypt when he leaves his wife
when he takes his daughter . . .
lex luthor was unjustly balded by superboy, superboy who
hounds him, belongs to a secret christian sect
who do not allow experimentation into the chemistry of life.
jimmie olson, superman's pal, is a homosexual.
when superman peers through you to see some spot far off
you get cancer, gamma radiation. his overhead flights
 are crumbling the masonry of metropolis. metropolis,
built on a fault. superman has a rare and sentimental collection
of everyday household objects he has stolen from open windows
                                            out of people's homes
jockstraps, small photographs of amputee sons who died
 in plane crashes. handkerchiefs, objects he has like a madman
 scoured the city for. the empty city.

dexedrine

the thing
  they cannot understand, how someone
  might want anything
    that much
with such craving. it scares them to think.
it endangers their lives immediately

   lives dependent on each other person
                             's predictability
and there is none of this
             not even
physical addiction. no arrests
     can be made
     that would guarantee
                   their being safe
    from this
intensity.
        from the intensity of the craving, also
they get a glimpse
          of money
     was has happened

            to them.

A roof & blankets

   pillow,
       dome
   / wadded around my
      head, like
   the tablecloth of a wound's

   painfeasting from

the pantry ,my awake mouthfuls are born from
are in most crude unchewable form, stored in

or a battlefield as quiet looking as Belgium
which only seems empty,when France & Germany ,between wars.
   stay continually full with French & Germans.

I have been thinking a great deal
about my bike that will be stolen.

I don't like things whose inevitability
works against me.

Why have you driven through my heart?
Make that   what.

O how becoming blind
mass becomes human
I can hear the city
breathing over my ears
I sheer like the table leg
    that folds under
cranes kiss wristwatch crystals
droop through the fog & rain like art nouveau
I stop and talk to a mailbox
I plan to talk
    to a police telephone
a cast iron human strolling in the dimness
the cab lets out
I turn around, kiss all the people whose daily
                  arms I am in
  and then swing around
      downhill to face the mist
  that cast iron pillar is accompanied
by a silent dog which is
  the shadow of a tree
  waiting for the day to walk it away.

Rope

Adoring the terrible speeds
I marry green to my flesh
we are ensconced in risk
During two glances
other things backgammon and
their lack of distance over the course
becomes painful and only meaningful seeing
the unmoving feet
cast iron ringed and bolted to the past
time is a sweep
a second takes the country in
the walls are what for a second remain, a second
holds and can't contain
adoring the speeds of whatever rides with it
I receive its favour as bride.
In this courtship fleeting green consumes me
constantly
and risk is strong enough
to build my life upon.
All things trail
my burning cold.

The colour of the moon has been getting me down
Something in the extrusive nature of both poetry and my body juices
makes this day as unbearable as a period

truly what it needs
the nearby bank

the thick copse
of its roots. In a sense

the lightbulb, airy
bodiless, unblue

is the opposite of dark green
avocado leafcentre.

socially drinking lightbulb light
at night

and occasionally, occasionally
by day, it thrives

and that's the way it goes, waiting
for a terrorist.

The credulous want response
I stare dull eyed literally pray
through this leaf. what white roots you have
avocado, I think
they are like the wanderings of an elephant's mind
on nitrous oxide on a dentist's chair
and does the plant
suddenly get greener, no
and if it's green enough does it
leap through the air
stretching its waistline
to grow good for my intentions, no
and while I go through
my peregrinations
do I doubt, of course, :I doubt
I concentrate the power of unwritten poetry
throughout my life on
to
that plant
and not even a scarred halffolded budtop unknurls the least
yet I must have faith;
It does not die in front of me..

If you are to go from my poems
or retire after the wealth our evenings revealed
-deposit any coin how small in th piggybank
of our mutual hallucinatory blend
then I'll have noticed each whisker
the evening bequeathed the morning
you'll have shrugged finally accepting
my baldness as if it were your condition
and are prepared to tell of me
to others you meet (whenever I am occasioned
to be landed like a struggling fish
upon the palate of your attentions,
my holidays , and corny botherings
that pull me forward (ever much dutifully
as I pull them after me) as I go on.

Called forth to don on the private occasion,
my ceremonial robes ,I confess, have
mildewed some —I am most reluctant
I leave the room of where things are
just content to happen unwritten up
as if I was being tried , knew the smell
and the word , the one word in my defense
didn't come , hesitated, wobbled about
the rim of decision , then,
like a basketball but not
a basket , rolled outward , offlipping.
I am called out by troubling , guilt
sheer loss rebounding backwards against
the echo of the first thrust's wave —I
am surprised , to be here to have found
myself so stopped so deadened — like
a man who stands arms by his sides
weeping in the midst of a volleyball game.

It is inobvious I will win. the small bore of truth
I squeeze it like a banana at the focus of a jungle

It is war I wage. the falseness within me against the individual.
Each battle of a war called time to make it human. I am drafted

I stand garbed in science fiction humour, a little behind my time
with weapons I can't understand   in my hands   at my hips

I cry through my banana like the failures of vaudeville
until later dawns and I die as a success because vaudeville
                                                has been withdrawn

reaching for something by which to retaliate   at life
I shoot my foot   I am not sure of the enemy   a whistle blows

and I am dragged off stage to be replaced
by some other idiot. it's cosmic,

more pockets are rifled
than merely mine.. yet-

am I to not take it all personally somehow ? this loss /
my failure.

I feel the night of a thousand clams.
let me, at the risk of being unromantic
advise our love dies a thousand times
while it is not born, because it is not.

you are my last meal. I put down my boomerang
to lament my bad toss and all is lost, you
are my last boomerang last glimmering hope, un-
romantically I see you: 'love on the hoof'.

The sky's pants is down; the virgin
has discovered drugs. The moon casts
wan light on syrups of a man's martini
and they were waiting for me
when I stopped. Creme de Menthe I yelled
   (using the american pronunciation) hasn't anyone here
heard the pope was seen in Florence on a mysterious
mission; mysterious like your eyes pale laundromat vision
I can win you with a coke
Men are throwing mistakes
off the back of a truck perhaps..
you are even one. They told him
but telling didn't do any good.
   what I don't like about you and what I don't like about
the Vatican are the same, tho..
   what I don't like about the vatican
less than contains you. you?   you remain,
aloof,
mysterious
bleeding on every doorsill
door jamb.

Dolores

Rejected by both Rimbaud and Verlaine
she felt as bad about it as Verlaine felt about Rimbaud.
Both Verlaine and Rimbaud however felt about it only as bad as
                                        Rimbaud felt about Verlaine.
This is horrible thought Dolores, rejected all my life.
She felt a little like Van Gogh's ear—
the *other* one.

Rimbaud felt badly too but about other things entirely
spurned by the muse at twenty, well, maybe 18
and still / Rimbaud all his life.   How/
would he live it down?

How would *she*? Well, Dolores still had a few aces up her sleeve
the ace of dildos/ the ace of comfort.
She lay back yawning and rubbed herself
the year was 1888. Closing her eyes

with her penchant for pornography
she conjured up a yet unpainted "Bathers" by Cézanne..

They looked foolish in black lace garterbelts
but no more foolish than Nixon in his oval office
and only half
as naked.

novella

because he was the one that suggested they might
be dishonest, because he was the one that would be, she
agreed, thinking only of him, he who only thought
of someone other than her. she wanted to be disloyal
only by being disloyal with him, to him, so when
he said: I did, did you (like we said we would) she
lied yes. he didn't really care, that wasn't really
the excuse he needed. he didn't really (need an excuse).
when she cried, he got angry; he said because she lied.

Pablo Geranium (largest guitar in the art world)
sidled over to Dolores (with a lanky stud's amble)
asked would she, was asked: would WHAT in reply
said Dolores as a preamble: cubist my eye, honey:square!
and she made the motion with her hands.

never saw such pussy at l'Estaque thought pablo
next time you sit on me and *I'll* go below
want mo', honey? askt Doloros to which
replied Pablo: sho'!

then they went over
to practeece with Matisse
whose wife
posed beside a brilliant persian rug next door
(Schukin brought the scene to Moscow to make Morosov jealous
:painter's wife cuckolded in a fauve surrounding"

the art world was silent
perhaps listening for war.

My brains tied to my belly by an unholy knot
I have always hidden them in a smile

entering the building that is woman

the form, so stretches over the skin from within.
each is as different as colour

In them, I am lost, like at every point of my life.

I am unable to see this colour/vibration except
 as something I come up against.   perhaps

deep inside hollow   where the fine elms all wrap
      together   and around eachother I feel
something further, required of me.

To search, to penetrate   to rub up against the mystery...
and then to not know what is expected of me !

Winter, I need your physical embrace. why ? -I am such spit on old
doorknobs. // when the dark isn't dark, but snowy, a bell rings
in the switchboard off both retinas. A drunk called 'endure' has
found an alley that is also a bar. he writes his name on the falling
porcelain, William Morris. O, once I was young and Rosetti..but soon,
I was in pieces like my heros. What I have wanted I have taken or been
taught. rejection slip from Artie Gold: Dear ...W.O.R.L.D...,

                        I am sorry but i have found yr poses
                        lacking in a certain 'awkward' grace
perhaps if you left them in the old urinal out behind............. or gave
them to a Monsieur...... they might bring joy to someone's heart. I
have found them not for me. Inelegant, unsentimental, unharsh. This is
the most difficult of these forms I have ever signed my.............. to,
                thankyou, I know you'll understand). .

Dec 6/7 77

Myth

I mean we'd be fucking and suddenly you'd
wince: pain, we'd be miles apart—where,
would that leave me. Say I'd be gently
raking the long of your back the back of a
fingernail, just so slightly, would snag
tear down your flesh . shudder. you'd jump
dear you would hit the ceiling. Flare up
like phosphorus   out of control in water
a different goddess you out of control in air.

I don't have the energy for another day
like a poor hand of scrabble without vowels...
the sun is at my throat

I wonder what sense I am making of human history
getting halfway through the day leave a poem   scrawk

just thinking about why I fail
screws me right in there
we have a sense of tradition

like watery spaghetti..

it is the poorer countries that I wonder about; there,
energy abounds. It is their gift to get ahead
to feel lousy doing it; mine
 to slip   and
to have one hell of a banquet:

  roast corpse of the western world. something must fill a hole—
or what is the dirt dying for?

I call this rarified morality
some days I can shoot it in my veins without my conscience flinching
these days I slide off without batting an eyelash.

A suspicion of death ? like a spy
send the heart / even into risk

    death lives near
        the allied sector
    death is no longer a citizen
    of death's country

    the heart is suddenly struck
like a safety match it
flares up like a tracer

the heart desires all it is denied.

    tying life

      life to time

    I grow out of opportunity
slippery my plastic guises

How can I feel the good guy
stopping my hand mid flight
giving it the rest of its life
  an average of 24 hours to any

statistically reckoning this guy
at the top of a curve of a bell
12 hours to grow mistakes
  12 hours to weed out others

until the *éphémère*'s
too senile to hold on to
its seaview its pier
 snapping off like a
            thrown camera
or an arc of ship sickled
in the handsome cabin boy

            hanged, swing
with no more than the dead one's
  heaving over wrists; spare
                 it what ?
spare me the shimmying out
  from under instant remorse
when my shrugs, protestations
attain a posture good worn
  below the webbed taut
ludicrous look and ten
fingers straining, contorting like
  one who is suddenly dealt
five poker cards in each hand
                 and
 left to children's puppets' audience

neither enjoying the winning as
  thing come as / a fortune better
nor the losing as fruit come from
  the tree of generosity's planning.

fruit ripe to rot in circle
about a careless toss from

(may as well be god's)/intended,(...-
as another's): so perfectly come/
to the circle's plotting centre.

How can you/
           hit a mayfly/
               why do you ? /
                        & you
/
do exactly what you're told to/
                    in Bolivia/
don't you ?
          /exactly what
          would the c.i.a.'s
          disinterest
          telecast ?
abandoning a thing they never had
             /   a hand in

a thing they held up for life rather than let the hand
  held to the left of their eyes
  mercifully maybe / chop out at

a hand just held against and away that way held harder
  constantly leaping the project's intention
like ideas how one would feel after lobotomy
  clearing up any gloom that might necessitate or
having seemed to ,
the operation .

what rules the country
is the thickness of small life

and greenery and the winds
of small invisible things

what rules the city, dogs
that are human beings.

what spoils the country
city things, dogs

that are human beings.
small flying things

detaching from the green
the rain of pollen

the plague of biting things
the things also

that ruin the picture of
the green.

things
that preserve the country

ghetto there in the roundness
of country ringing city

things
that are ringed

won't give themselves up
to the noose.

you

leaning, like a Hardy Boy
I touch my fingers lightly
to the invisible panel

if I listen, *fear* falls away
how are you ? over, the green hills
the panel swings, revealing-

revealing summer. daylight
roars from the spot. Above me
you stand like an easel

I lean my face sideways
tenderly towards you, nuzzle,
like an artist who has lost his brush

and what he'd begun to do
bending over, *was simply to retrieve it*
and then, *he fell in love with an idea...*

I, across from her
she coy to the point of almost
inviting me. From where I sat

extending silence
stretching it to the point it almost
must be done. In my mind

I have allowed myself
the freedom of dining together, already
she has probably thought.

Nothing of the sort,
just considered me. Head to toe,
another stranger. I strangle

my thoughts, inventing
churches, crazy banquet halls, where if anyplace
had she envisioned me? Then,

she gets off the bus, I
start with embarrassment. Realize no one
saw me thinking.

My pants are a drawer for my feelings
your mind is a shower curtain for your feelings
we stand in the same room
changing

if nothing was to happen in autumn
why would the wind enter the woods

niceday

It's such a nice day   we have lunchmeats &
wonderbread delivered by a boy we tip a quarter
take from drawers of kitchenettes on 12th floors
gladbags napkins   , brown paper bags & cloth table spreads
and knock on a friend's door who lives on the
same floor as we do in midtown Manhattan &
invite him for a picnic in the fields of Far
Rockaway an elevator & subway ride only
away from the hustle & highaltitude & stovecookt food
like a man who with one foot kicks his garagedoor
closed behind him while he pushes in front a whirring
hungry lawnmower, we head for the grass just outside the Bronx.

I have no astrologer-
and don't believe in falling in love
on any particular August day you could name

I have knapsacks full of knick-knacks
that spread beneath a tree
would suffocate a hermit

and a perpetual cough
that when I've had enough of-
I'll die from.

I came to this city
naked   and from a small town
and have rearranged some of its objects

I will hitch-hike out of here one day
with my hair in my eyes and a good breeze blowing
and cause a little confusion I'm sure-

though no more than a hair
discovered in a gravy.

made up dream

red matchheads frozen into clear ice
the coachman whipping his horses
their quivering nostrils
what they smell
the bat outlined against the moon the moon
outlined against the trees
the trees outlined against the sky
the sky outlined against the forest
the eerie light
the very yellow automobile yellower
than any i had ever entered
the sudden sickening of my heart at the smell
i wondered was this insanity
the voice from the front seat
driving.

So many things remind me of you
The birth of christ: Georges de La Tour(around 1633)
page 126 Art news Annual/1955 :The Repentant Magdalene
a nude, Kirchner painted. A Matisse
something by Berthe Morisot
that Lehmbruck in The Boston Museum
the body of a modigliani
things Picasso was fond of saying
the first cubist painting
Les Demoiselles d'Avignon—
-a picture I once jerked off to.
Though Art resounds with your images today,
my life has lost the realness of your touch.

I am no bargain but I like snappy service
what were you doing when you were not paying attention to our
love? I tell you, neither was I, I mean—
I started to.. but then, you
were looking away, so I looked away
and I didn't see anyone but neither
        did I see you looking at me so
I kept looking away. you know—
like those streetcorners where everyone
 is looking up
because
  the first person
looked up ?

I yell at you
and you cry at me
and overhead
all the time
the neighbor's big boots clomp
and you cry
and I know
though I can't hear you
walking down the hall I'll
open the door
suddenly
be confronted
with the whole sad sorry replay
there
on your
stomach in tears
dry gutwrenching
thousandth time performed ritual
and to what avail
Do things get better
do things
get worse
All above the while
pound the neighbor's big
clumsy black boots
like the heartbeat of some long viking oarship
we both are tied-to doomed to row
forever and ever.

1 for Kina

What you are most afraid of will never happen
would never happen
what you are left with subtract your fear
which can't happen
is what you most want to happen to you
between which I
and your fear stand alternately, 0, and minus 1
like the only 2 solutions to some quadratic equation.
and of course while you do nothing
all there is to regret in this world occurs to me, the
Easter Parade of our sad miscalculations, all the
things we never got and kept wanting marching beside
all the things we thought would be worth having and weren't.

I am sorry, muse, for the difficulty
with which I am drawn. My trip towards you
is not man's towards god, no, mine

and I am sorry but in the abstract
not sorry for what I have already done
though it is so little, sorry, for what I

might have and hadn't. didn't want to do,
didn't. for the grace of my reluctance for
the fullness of the protests, these. these

were real   and did embarrass   and continue
I am used to you, my strange old ways; then
not   that has become an action in itself

sometimes I feel I have jumped over to the other side
and with my own damned sword I fight beside all
those natural obstacles: a defector against my own self.

More things interrupt my work
than carry it on, yet
some things do carry it on. I
open letters, see a note on
the night kitchen counter—
a dear friend of the dear friend
that I live with has died
is to be buried tomorrow
and the phone rings while I am reading
and on the phone is my mother and her
brother, my uncle has died and he also
must be buried. neither of these deaths
affect me but they
affect those closest to me
I am being
buzzed by death. my companions' companions
go down
and they worry about me
and I feel like the body in a hammock
tied both sides onto two trees and no
tree I am tied to
touches me. In the centre
 I swing
sideways, while death
moves on
ahead. I feel my marvelous life, untouched
and I skirt both boards on a narrow runway.

my life seems full of holes
that come together only in sadness
it is as a blindman
will sell pencils, rethrush chairs
that I write poetry , Intuitively ,
joylessly with a sense
of no industry
and constant partial loss
no longer to deal with a crisis
perhaps no longer even to put one off
just lay the stuff down
and have it criticized while I don't listen
and when it is all over to leave
and when it is all over to leave
like a cake placed in a two hour oven
in a building with a bomb. not caring.

uncontestably you are overdue
jazz blares in an empty livingroom
to greet you, messiah

somewhere a bubble rises questioningly
-are any of us ready for the air ?
I go see what the jazz attracts, what moths.

and you aren't there. whatever you are
your not being there tells me nothing of.
I thirst for the first drink.

Giraffes burn
apples have hats
a child lifts a lake to get his ball
either a grinning cat or a horsefaced horse plays fiddle
but seldom am I so relaxed
as when
I read a Maigret.
something Simenon is doing...

cuticles skip ropes
the winds of a year
blow off the pages of eternity
in the face of time

the grass burns
torn by autumn

red hair

tears, kerchiefs soaked together
my youth chopped down like a young pear tree
the coconut souring

the mountains worn away
and I still live by the river.

The Beautiful Chemical Waltz

Selected Poems

(The Uncollected Poems)

lovingly for
Geoffrey Young
and Candy Schwartz
who know why

"let's go   a'   twilight fishing
me too ,   you too. . "

Chuck Berry
ca '64

SELECTED GOLD

For a medium-sized city, English-writing Montreal has always been the home of a lot of poets, and quite a few interesting ones. English-writing Montreal is not Paris, so it is not the centre to which the homeless trek; it is not often the place where the latest poetry occurs. It has its own traditions and its own histories. In Montreal, for instance, there have been enough Jews writing poems in English to keep a medium sized country going for a century or two.

Many of Canada's most famous poets have to be identified with Montreal: A.M. Klein, for instance, Irving Layton, Leonard Cohen. For a few decades in the middle of the century English-writing Montreal was a place where pretty important literary movements and debates took place. I think that there are probably still people in cafés who are picking sides between John Sutherland and Patrick Anderson.

In the seventies and eighties a bunch of young poets, like many of their predecessors immigrants to Canada, laboured to create a poetry movement gathered in the building and cognomen of the Vehicule gallery/press. The publisher of the present collection was a member of the group. So was the editor of the present collection. The author of the present collection was the group's Arthur Rimbaud.

Ses strophes bondiront : Voilà ! voilà ! bandits !

A hundred years after Rimbaud wrote his first poems and landed in his first jail cell, I was teaching creative writing, as they called it, in Montreal. Naturally, quite a few students I sat with have gone on to publish poetry, but none of them at the time read as much poetry as did A. Gold, as he then signed himself, with the possible exception of his friend Dwight Gardiner. I was delighted to find that Artie had read Jack Spicer and Frank O'Hara especially, and that he thought of them when he wrote his own stuff. At that time the established Montreal poets, and the vast majority of the would-be poets, did not read Spicer and O'Hara. My fellow professors had never heard of them.

But Artie had, and that is how I knew that he was serious about poetry. He was not interested in getting famous or expressing his uniqueness or preparing himself for a job teaching creative writing. (Artie never chased any kind of a job very hard.) He wanted to know what was happening at the front end of the arts. What I noticed in 1970, and what keeps coming through his poetry, is his learning, his engaged reading of the avant garde. Unlike too many of his peers, he really knew what surrealism was, and he also understood the history of glass art, for example. A tremendous collector, he had an apartment crammed with geodes, art-deco lamps, Arthur Rackham illustrations and insolent cats:

you could have seen his silhouette
leaping like a made up mind
across balconies
below streetlight moons

Late night halloween superhero Artiepoet. For Gold the image is what the human mind can do. Reference is not as important as utterance, or maybe we should say that when it comes to skewing one, it will be reference. In this way Artie Gold is not Arthur J.M. Smith.

Spicer and O'Hara reminded their readers that poetry is made of speech, and speech can be exciting no matter the subject. In other words a young poet doesn't have to write about suicide or seduction to be interesting.

In fact smart-talking poetry corporal Gold was, in my opinion, just what the seventies needed. We had a lot of younger lyricists consolidating their post-language territories, solemnly dishing out free-verse stanzas on the northern experience or immigrant families toughing it on the plains. Gold is a city poet for sure, wielding lingo instead of a Canadian agenda:

So many things remind me of you
The birth of christ: Georges de La Tour(around 1633)
page 126 Art news Annual/1955:The repentant Magdalene
a nude, Kirchner painted. A Matisse

Since his first poems Gold has always shown taste. He has sometimes given in to a weak impulse, to be another poet entirely, a tabloid cantor or something. But withal he is an erudite collector of history's hippest poets — in that way he was usually ahead of his peers, reading Mayakovsky when they were reading something from their high school textbook or *Rolling Stone*. They were likely listening to some two-chord guitarist, while for Artie a quiet influence might be Charles Ives:

just the gentle old man
thinking and humming
beside a piano river.

The point is that Artie learned good and early that he wanted to live in a world populated by such figures. For him culture was not that thing the vulgarizing anthropologists have made it, whatever society makes and does. Culture was what our artists refined. Not that Artie went around in velvet suits, carrying a scented hand-kerchief to his nose. "My muse must be a neighbor with/a street address," he wrote. That's just fine, because while he seems to be saying that his poems will be filled with actual and motley big-city detail, fig newtons and slippery porch-steps, he is also here violating the territory, plunking a chunky hipster beside the Pierian Spring.

All this while most of the wide-scattered Canadian poets have never entertained the notion of asking the muses for anything. They think that they can "express themselves" in tidy anecdotes about spouses in bed or toddlers in the autumn leaves (I have just glanced at a typical Canada Council L.C. Poets quarterly).

One hears that Artie Gold does not conduct a particularly safe life, either, but I wouldn't know for sure. I know that his lines are not something I, for instance, would dare walk across Niagara on. He takes chances. So while he can somehow invest an accurate and homely image with great sadness, "the tumbler lying on its side on the darkened rug," he can also take risks that fling a kind of pleated reality at you: "In the soft plaid mesquite/ she extends her arms to me."

He has a daring ability to objectify his voiced poem by starting a new one this side of it:

I have been thinking a great deal
about my bike that will be stolen.
I don't like things whose inevitability
works against me.
Why have you driven through my heart?
Make that what.

Are we listening to him and therefore wondering about the written? Or are we reading and suddenly seeing a second-last draught as perfectly polished speech?

I don't know what A. Gold does now, but he used to write a tremendous number of poems, huge shaggy piles, more and more of them, pushing for the apogee, where there might be more poetry than life, when the impossible crashes down and it turns out that his life will be his major poem, the comprising of all those fragments. He tried to shore up the world itself with his fragments, I thought. Think.

Now in the most recent poems here he has done what I ask of all serious writers younger than I — he has developed a poetry I have a hard time following. I remember David Bromige plainly stating that he had gone into poetry because it was difficult to understand. The difficulty is a gift of which I am glad. I am also glad to have known this fridge-emptying, quarto-filling poet, newly middle-aged, I suppose. He was the first person who called me GB, now my signature.

— *GB*
Vancouver, '91

I wrote by an open window
I don't know why
I thought of having all the Archipenkos
in the whole world
sort of as a replacement
for a woman I need but can never find
as if one were anything like the other
one I need and would like to have
the other I need and cannot
I thought of my need going into
                                    this room
as I rounded steps to get here.   there
all the women were
in essence:
the music in the elevator;
I could not reach it to turn it off.
I rounded flights of stairs
coming closer, straying farther   /
from where I could not reach it
Sometimes I wonder what is inside
                                    a rock
   what crystals   what hollowness
   what solidness   /   what
                              disappointment
often when I am feeling
                  an orange
                  in my hands
   I think: need this orange have seeds ?

like two penguins fighting over a scrap of plastic
who ever arranged the city   ?   It is just there absurd
as the area of human interest, narrow like some south pole
and what a mosh the concept of the soul somewhere along
someone has gotten a wedge of pride into the spirit. it
is like some banana peel, slippery fatal. it will floor it
   I look beyond the winter white the mammoth growls of
                              tractor
I look beyond the winter night
   I look into the character of the llama as if it were
a camel, you yell at me: incorrect; ahhh. but I'd had such
                              hopes for the soul.
   do pickles ionize in the brine barrel   ?
that is the courseness of the swim; each generation spawned
must forget.   me, oh, I lean out of life as if it were a window
                              yawn.
and what grows out from must always to protect its trunk
tuck its leaves in
and what it grows among must for the sake of complaint
   remind it to:
   perhaps change is a rebellion against the phases of some
                         monotonous drear.
brer human brer weakness brer frailty of spirit brer human
                         witness to forget?

'g' as in Gold

Who am I to stand and demand   ?
failure is my lesson.   failure and refusal.
I withdraw from the flame
my hand.

And cold, who am I to not want
the warmth of the flame, the flame that is woman.   I want.
the affection
the attention.
Living life does more than *prove* to me.

I never look past an act for that act's pleasure
so why isn't the world contained by my glance of it

This malarial life we feel cold we feel hot
the order of sensations confuses us
our blankets are as clumsy as our decisions
and we must doctor ourselves against our own cures.

'g' as in Gold

Who can I redress ?
only I understand me.
I want to start over in some city in my mind.
the tomb of the man who threw up.

who will not meet me: the world
who I will not meet
I gaze at its steel.   It
has the advantage.   Myself pressed against it
is the sharpness of the blade.   Myself
pressed against it is my *need.*

This desperacy, a clumsiness   I affect;
Women see me coming, no one stands due/ before
a love that is blind. Those who volunteer
do so for the risk
and not for me.

qu'ode

I am aware of my intolerances as do my perfections
blow off into the night / I only ask you / to consider me kindly
as change is full of worlds, somewhere there I am loved
even by you
memory disinherits bitterness, a distant memory
disinherits impatience even striving towards that act.
that something you have to love to anchor yourself into the world:
let be *me.*
when you say the *body* of a rabbit you turn it sideways
do me some such kindness. a forced passion perhaps. I
will reiterate (at times love is only mechanical
even stolen from the physical act.

garlic in the coffee doesn't work—why should it
but, it works better than shaving with a pistol
and why is *that* ?
it must be that the statement is one of those of
the kind / if everybody read Poetry there'd be no war—
(of course there'd be no Prose *either.*
which doesn't work in only one of a million ways something might
(not.).
it has been a year of opposite effects
we used to buy things we couldn't afford
and bring them home in a taxi
now the rifle sights of the new budget
have brought all this to a standstill,
like one caress will, a cat.
We find ourselves on an unsure hill
all our strength & better natures
niggling, before its uninvestigated slope.
The blues is not in fossil preservation I decide.

"V"

Hurrying to spill what I had
like a man who was writing a phonenumber
across the cover of a book— where was I
grinding a world at a wheel down to a
substantive.   Romantically I thought
what might I part with
to twin miseries if also I couldn't
have you   ? you, you through
my eyes— viewed romantically
something I hungered after, outerfire
necessary for the consuming allocated
my life — viewed as one might
a chicken one has backed up against
the bare boards of barn .   If then
I could have had you automatically
I would have had to reject
that lack of suffering.   If then
I would have had to reject you
for that to just amount to that
I think somehow I & I would have
been cosmically for a second, squared.
Oh good foolishness O craziness
going on in the countinghouse.

The Relativity of Spring

I

The nouns are hungry for sense
The facts are not known
They are tasteless by which is meant
They are hard to transcribe
They taste the colour of the sky against cement
They appeal slightly as apples might
and their bodies crawl like turtles with shells
and they fall taking sun to the ground on them.

Yipping like dogs they crawl being blistered in the sun
on the back of the dolphin a caress touches like an alarm
cancer of the colon, the skin
tendril of the bone's sensuality.

The dark dirty dishwater of an x-ray plate
The queen's love throws the first pitch
It reveals the hidden
It sings into activity
telling garbage from submerged fish
and dreams

Water's sudden edge
bell's flower
for the sun to be useful to its breathing
for the sight who loses sequence in art
he comes up with what chemicals it will provide
she watches her replacement
we the complex lobster wearing animal pelt
we the gods describe this earth totally
where the sharks can never really come is totally our own
where this takes place is our authority

The air's barely acceptable sending of sound
The queen's idea throbs like starmatter
no one wasting words outside of speech

no one worries hard stone
the surprise in one's voice not heard from passing back to oneself.
The boards of the palace are grained.

II

I dance like air in autumn
I house like shadow
mercenary of breath
shortcircuiter of meadow
Each season I arrange orthogonally
Each semicircular jar I denote pleasurable
In the marketplace of chrome dwarfs
In the ring of deserts
In the feelings of scorned women reaching out to trap this society
The whips of each jealousy reaching chords deeper than music
These days are hard to endure going through submarine time
These policemen strike into fear itself

I am the cauldron of bowling prowess
I am the crying one who is struck
I am greatness whose ass even pirates must kiss
and I am exactly worrying, hesitation
The double versatility of early intent
The pompous exultant baboon
was like a mastery aced
was like a spectacle too ugly to behold
before dying it shook my hand like three tired popes
before dying it strutted pretending to thank me
The passport is subject to unholy fits
The mountain is climbed sorrowfully
Get here this moment on your knees
Go out slowly but towards joy
crawling along the broken glass of your mistakes
a cautious second life
No one has to love life even
just to continue living.

III

Now come through a beating of pasts
born so as to miss my vote.
It is when through a slant that it begins with bitter purity
and by some chance bitching gets it a poetry
into pallid flung arms they boldly set to
coming full circle in some mind's interchange
and each comes into an encampment of its own.
With its arrival the year is splintered into ten thousand months
To kill something aleatory from my bitter cache
thinking perhaps by this action to arrive at one spring.

It is certain the typed characters dog in shame
fuses follow them like tails, hissing in guilt
before which cult I bear greetings of change
the necessary amount of steps must be walked
we are as wanted as any drug
as dangerous as two colds from one source.

"A-12"

The scraping of ladders about the blue day haze
a forceful scarlatti   , somewhere an increasingly meddlesome coronet
the day unfolds   a mailman rifling slots   jamming mail thru with
    his arm
a bite about to be bitten into a sandwich someone holds up to the air
gazing admiringly at a slip of lettuce as if it were a petticoat
neruda on my desk alive in poems dead somewhere buried in Chile
the day does the living a deep honour
memory and concern tunnel through its myriad distractions
love for you like a light / flickering on a jukebox half-plugged-in
prints itself as delicately on my consciousness as lipstick on a forehead
so much damage done by the waiting but it all serves like commas
finally to have been valuable not merely annoying

Blue Thought

Now listen to the Honegger of street noise
one particular aspect you'd never before separated

standing there   watching her cab disappear   thinking of
garbage trucks—why?!

Always it is there.
Listening harder you can hear behind it
but it is a music.
                    Wind playing with a shaft of light
falling through the sky with gravity. Am I sane?—
why?!
at times . . .

Nothing for the hands
so they fall back at my sides.

When a door closes you stand   the words
suddenly like a meadow before you
the cabin behind like a desert you have thought yourself out of
                                            not crossing.

What sleep parts to   /   that isn't waking
that inner space
at sea that surrounds the boat
and is not the water   /   in the same
way   /   that you are not
the boat

but on land is always a semicircle before
in a trembling dome above and ahead
you are afraid to clear your throat
as if god were standing there
and you had no idea what he wanted—perhaps
total silence of you

and rain starts across the sky like a mission   in the far mysterious east
a large hand of it
slapping the hills.

Three Seconds of Understanding

It is perhaps because I cannot understand my youth that I
can relate it. The battle between what I did do, and common sense
now, that tells me *that was right or wrong, does not exist* ; instead,
that battle exists as fractionated difficulties in the world today,
contradictions in my soul, the understanding of where I am and what
I must do, with, no idea of why it is so difficult. Habits like
vague recurrent failures;   rarely working for our success. Meaning we
must amend our positions constantly, restate our logic for its poor
workings.

Then, we hardly dared accept; now, dare we not question the
mechanisms that support a thousand escapes?

Someone is trying to save us from drowning but can that person
swim? Are we drowning or will we only be drowning if we go after our
selves? There is something narcissistic about all this neurotic at-
tention. We may throw ourselves in after ourselves and drown in lakes
the size of private wells. These elevator shafts are our hells. We
have no caution, sized out by Romance.

The milkbottles rattle and my day begins. Sneaking in I lay
down twelve quarts of shame and crawl into the bedroom of my dis-
affiliation. I am more afraid of the boss phoning the house than of
the husband bursting in.

Ode to Focal Shifts
for Stephen Rodefer

'Brilliant but erratic' . . . like
                    the heart
                              on speed

but aiming for that continuity, the most   'mosts',
I rode down St Dominic   south
                              from Marianne
            the young shrieks
            of little girls
            are as rosebuds :
            the Spring's

      a curious blue
      the colour of traveller's checks
      suffuses the sky
"I keep the smell
                    of my burning
                    neighborhood
                    in mind"

the sad arpents of
            quebec
                    — or
      do just I
            think so ?
            any *less* so   in the city ?
you   would   think so /   but no . . .

      sometimes, as if then didn't wind
                              into
                        now
I wish it was a long time ago.
      however (luckily)
      what it is all about
changes from day   to day. just as when you say:

      " we
      live in a GLIDDEN house, 'paint',
      becomes *Christly.*

I wish she had been more pleased at the onset
to see her now definitely less fitfully sleeping
the wry grin and smugness I am denied consciously of

blame a deposition before conscious ability
no wealth surely in keeping it in
but I want just the same to keep it in

I am not sure of the bonds that ravel us secretly
when both of us are finally asleep
beyond the gravity and heavy responsibility of knowing
something delights to possess

there the moonbeams and subtler emotional creatures
tiptoe to some collective joy that it wears like relaxed muscles
in a body asleep.

a night w Astri

Resources

The freedom duplication of resources guarantees
but my one hand in your one hand when we walk . . .

I will be blunt; what love/
has not brought me to my knees? At least love
like some dream of plenty, mercurially gathers all into its meniscus
—shall we walk around any such granary without complete possession?

away from you
I become philosophical . . .
which is like taking off one's glasses to *see.*

R.W. 1

You've been willing to love me.
I've been high-handed and heavy, a fool,
believing what we had was perishable
I was all around it with my protective hands—
a fool. I smothered it. I think I put the flame out
every time you fought to keep it alive
and I don't think you thought it was me you were fighting.
and I've done it before with others.

I'm a bit afraid to act for I've seen all the clumsiness
the ineptitude of my dealings with women.
If I treat them differently,
I treat the situations all the same. Smothering them. Now love's

not a thing I am afraid to see grow. Not something I fear—
not in the least. Love is something I am dying without.
I have squeezed promises at the cost of lying
going home I should have known
you can't extort love. Why I wanted to
I'll never know how it came to pass that I made such harsh demands.

What wasn't she giving
to me that I wanted something, what was left to want—
now I am a man who doesn't know again if ever he will try,
nor enjoys the thought of eating, sleeping, healthy walking.
I want to slide on my knees into some open corner and be small
and wait.

R.W. 2

Beauty will drink a toast at my wanton destruction (an event) /
disclosing the cumbersomeness of my race like a rotting commode
a tractor tries to outdistance / but is chained to by blood.

Had we this. had we that.. imploringly we feed.   I should have loved
your double standard . . if need could invent love;   here we have
/ bad blood / here we dream. Sending monsters into our Tokyo.
The sun sets against the idea of caves thinking to have found a ledge.
In the mornings . . Mozart and Villon,   the singular of caress, *cares* . .

We think we have stumbled on the sudden and secular secret that will
     just for us   unlock worlds,   well, won't it?   the morning runs off
and like an oxbow lake small life is stranded in these stagnant pools
the blood in our minds, goes stale while the salt of life without /
     even becoming precious, concentrates to burn us where we've chosen
                                                  to make our stands.

Zvia— come see me . . .
The jets
      trace lonely circles through the air
high above, they make no noise . . .
I am poisoned down here
      the exhausts of buses early in the afternoon
      the afternoon painted in arrested circles against the sky
the pigeons die in this city, fly low through each lane
      separate city canyons . . . I wait for you
a ring at a phonebooth I pause hesitantly at before passing
traffic yawns, swallowed by the city . . . I am lost
the few trees here remind me
the few robins here remind me
the streets my friends live on, counted on my left hand
      I hold it ah high against the sky
the diffused sun, reminds me
the impossible hour
reminds me. There is so much I don't know . . .
      are you coming?
      What can I be sure of ?

R.W. 5

Love is the thread that sews
two people together
into short theatric rows.

Love is the designer
the audience grows
people in bunches get love together
like faith.

Love does to the individual
the florists' intent
intent on selling wholesale retail.
Love swells the heart
and the heart enters love's passage

probing uncertainly
one thrill can kill love
at some early stage

like fucking the immediate family
it steals the pleasure of
enterprise

and love can die
In the time it takes a highrise
to become a slum.

R.W. 6

If her heart never leaks the information
that I must assess occasionally
and no distance can inform in confidence
then she spills her feelings for no one, for no one else is about
so I cannot see her while she is this, and this struggling
perhaps my feeling that she comes from the pieces together again
is again late and then she is down again and
it could be mocking if I joked about these things,
secular hardships going unnoticed until I poked
and then the poke is a cleat
and ugliness pops its head out
laughing
at the futility of good intention.

R.W. 7

Why suppose the heart is not actually broken
tiptoe past the mirror of a lit room
seeing but not actually dealing
I have lost control say and a queen reposes face down in my pile
among the flurry of hearts I have taken in
all but one: and? there are thirteen.
They come in in twos and when you have given six you have made twelve
and one left over therefore there being two piles
the pile with your hearts
and the pile with theirs.
Now can you hear the singular ring cleanly escape the possessive's
mystique? In other words, I was playing solitaire
and I will not tell the world if my heart is broken or not
for now. And for now / life goes on. Now, tell me my heart—
is that one cliché— or two, stuck-together?

R.W. 10

I leaned into her eye
took inventory of both pockets
I told her
I couldn't fix a broken heart right now

but if she'd come back
(if she'd go away)
I'd write
and poems are the greatest balm my soul knows

then I released her wrist
and left her in London, England,
stole off back to Canada
like a midnight pretender. Pretending

her eyes weren't warm enough for both of us
her wrists were white, calcine
but I'd write her
as the hopeless yell at angels to be blessed

I bargained for my soul with that witch
and cried on the plane that brought me home
necessary tears, while I clutched
my birth certificate.

R.W. II

These are the trappings of my world,
these are what I do.
Gathered, a print or two, a vase—
a thousand urgent books
stacks of magazines
forgotten
the hallway stretching between enthusiasms
like a referee—
unwestern,
what I am but also
a little western, wanting
to be what I am not. The things,
speak for me obviously, not for themselves, flung
haphazardly in the space of neat living
I carve out like the innards of some festive turkey,
that, my life, carved, eaten, transferred
to the belly. It is in the gut I live, just as light
dwells in the crystal of its chandelier
more than in the room . . .

R.W. 12

My sanity as an external thing
I focus on say a twig that looks like a frog
but I want it to be just a twig
if twig it is
yet I see it always as a sort of 'striving to become
a frog'
it exists
in the bubble zone. Not saying my sanity is something
in a lane I've driven by
bricked up
entombed in some uncertain back
of no, definite address, no.
I have waved to my body passing it on a freeway
and it, often, was going the other way
against me: I would feel pierced
but the world is not set up that way.
Not exactly—
the game of control is more like shaving in a mirror
or cutting hair, watching as I do the wrong thing the mirror
do the right. All through the night
I have stood, craning my neck,
my body twisting, one sun going down
bringing up another
and exhausted I have been delivered unto the morning
rather hairless, a sight,
my bald eyes sprained,
pains in my elbows where they have reached around to hold the scissors
a good feeling, another opposite
implanted in me from that harrowing night.

R.W. 13

The green buds nod on, the cars,
horn, vying for arterial position
the sun smiles a little kittenishly at first
then lets whip loose on the tongues of the sunshine trees;
exhausts twin along the throughway, neatly like two
    ferrets disappearing simultaneously down
      two ferret holes
and I itch wandering out in the morning glare.

It's so white it seems nothing's out there yet—
but *I* am.

R.W. 14

A log of your not being here:
A hundred dollars is stolen from my bedroom by a friend
the cats kill the tomato plant
the bean plant dies
the big cat catches cold
the small cat follows suit
I take the change from your piggybank
and the stamp from your desk
a longdistance phonecall to Miami
some money comes
I replace what I took
I run out of what I replace during the weekend
the white sugar is gone the milk sour
the taps run the doorbell doesn't work
the kitchen fuse goes
I feel I need you
more and more.

R.W. 15

She leaves the radio on for the plants
but that's all she does for the plants.
Later she cannot even meet the power-bill.
The plants have taken everything
and died.

R.W. 16

We fence with the unknown
or perhaps
we merely flex our this and that in any case
I am left
the area of presumption wholly mine . . .

I draw you because that is what you do and by it
I seek your approval
but after, after nothing, I write about you also—
and you
go home . . .
but I do too.

R.W. 17

As in that first mouthful of some hybrid
I am gazing at your new colour you are
wrapped in tissue like a nectarine
my bicycle rides on your surface
I hold my breath
not like the mouth dealing with celery
certainly not like the sound of me
travelling over ordinary gravel
has it rained between myself
and life
to produce you?
Your weakness embarrasses me,
displays you in a horrid light
will I have
like the radio
to pass over you
hand on the mighty dial of this world my neighborhood ?

R.W. 18

Now the night streets fill with rain
cloying thoughts of youth sweet fill me
a time when all was perfect.

The sugars of uncertain peanut candy
the dusty powder sprinklings handed over the counter
the sad old lady's face, bright
gleam of the copper pennies twenty years ago.

The fruit smell of Succoth
the granite over-large passagehalls
chanting recitatives of school:
music to the ear.

Winter comes, unreasonably
I am struck, here,
in the middle of my life.

R.W. 19

A nest of gleaming silver on the jet wing
below is land or coastline or solid ocean
blue white silver white magnesium white

clouds exhaust without vehicle I dream
each is a dolphin happy chasing after us
dry half; bodies warm as I am snug inside

tangent to Magellan dotted lines axes
hardly moving slow earth turning over
like a tractor rotor gainer handstands

sweet hard candy lens knocked shuddering
hands drill cigarettes all lengths to screw ashtrays
flaps pound we shake we travel through what we make.

R.W. 20

First I sought silence
then I sought to unfocus the mirror
I had made an enemy in the passage

above a slatternly pizza joint lit
by a one-fifty bulb above 10 greek drivers
above the other consciousness that I had escaped

climbing
those rickety stairs
there was a gleam a surface
in the toilet bowl
I couldn't piss away that external
                              reflection

my eyes docked at a thick waterpipe
clumsy with ten thick coats of paint
nothing would hide its shape really
but everything above its actual self
kept threatening to.

I thought of the sun
creeping up on a bank
                of clouds
unzipping and waving its sunshine
dappled syrups on us humans
ten stories below.

Poem

Still there was a chance of you coming to the party
I shaved threw on my best smile
mischief is external to us
subtle tampering with my dime while I/
am in a phonebooth thinking all is swell
it is — isn't it ? true mischief
camouflages in with the very grain of life
or how grim I should have felt that casual night.

The magician doesn't draw kerchiefs voilà voilà no.
The kerchiefs are knotted together like
the bedsheets of an escaping prisoner. He lowers
the length endlessly before your vision . . . the lines of
a good poem come like that.
How long that is
your hopes riding on the lowering end cannot ascertain
knotted to the bent window bars of the cell window
you cannot tell when it will end seeing it passed
verse by verse inside out past the beginning gripped
somewhere in some stage of the middle.

R.W. 22

You know I know there is not much point getting interested in poetry
for *my* sake I will die . . . and not leave you the business.

R.W. 23

How can there be poems about anything
not clogged with you
not choked with you?
I say
this is how I live meaning
this is not how.
I say I don't want ever to see you again meaning
I can't wait for that next time.
I see sleep
think
in opposites.
I am a jellybean
outside the bag.
Life shines blue lights on me
red lights
soft, pink lights
light green
yellow
light blue
naked
under the streetlight
set up for a Gene Kelly routine
I await you,
let us dance, Ginger.

R.W. 24

I kiss her fever
pedal by on my bicycle
she interrupts her fingers'
downtown sky's horizon
she runs furrows broad
down me turning
   squint against the sun

from a phonebooth where a
door folds under her arm
she could walk away with
                  my
heart
      while I shoot a light and car-horns &
                           pedestrians
                           finger me . . .
(—me, whose blush spells
                  refreshment.

R.W. 25

too awful if
your love for me is merely a weakness I prey upon
the point of love is lost somewhere in living
art's trace vanishes invisibly while
the science of living
abruptly perverts.

R.W. 26

Down your back love railroads must be built
finger trains to traverse in the night
love lighting the network
in the night skies of my room
coming upon a breast
it will glow like a city
my brain
the transformer of your heart.

R.W. 27

The silhouette is
a literary device

I thought till I
saw you lined up

against the night
sky/ then I thought:

the moon
is a flashlight.

Postcard

Hello from the world's
                tallest building.
           I can't shake
the beginnings of depression.

R.W. 28

Deeper than a notebook's surface
but not faster than America
I wonder about our love: what is it?

In this package of skin,
I amuse myself by amusing you.

Love is notorious!

THE HOTEL VICTORIA POEMS

3 interfaces of black / light knocks at

I have frightened her
one up
and still I go one
up to her
she who
may not even like
myself
live on that floor
on which we first
met
but
have herself
descended
as I could have, not
ascended, as I did.

dec 29/30. 76

*

there is the pipe smoke
that is like plankton in water
it is proof not only I
thread bare hallway rugs in slippers
I have seen 2 girls there
one watching the other
the other watching the one
the both watching me
as I turned to go
by some silent consensus
one spoke , they both spoke
said – hi! (like –
snappy!)
and sometimes the phone rings
that is in the morning. one night
a hand, pausing on its way
down the long hallway, for a second
felt my doorknob
but it was not my hand
so it went on, on to its own.
like a waterfall behind a lightswitch
things wait there just out of reach.

jan 6.77

*

what speed in my veins what desire
what cold breath descending down
upon the buttercup the glacier
what impossible odds all the silences
what pencil of wind my small voice
disturbing what vast stillness
what is to be
and yet what
desire. what hope. what sounds
just in listening what great
tradition previous to me   what
momentum says I do , maintains.

jan 9.77

*

like the petals of the chrysanthemum
one by one the events of this evening
lead me to the evening's middle :
    which is ,   quiet
                thought/
                at its end .

    the two dollars of cab driver who
was
    talking the whole world was stupid
I remember we passed the Royal
    Ontario Museum and I thought :
closed . The bastard is locked
                out of Art .

The growling
    of a snow melting machine
        somewheres
    outside of my hotel window

the conversations with the night
    desk clerk
    down in the darkened lobby .

His name was Brian   he thought
    me strange — my name is Artie
I thought
            him strange - O !
    which of us is strange ?

do you know , glass-collie , glass
collie I saw in a window going
home to my day's middle .

jan 10/11.77

*

The immeasurable charm of having
something I have not — nothing
seems like the flu, totally un-
desirable . I measure my syllables
like a man who owns
a vast chert-field — he knows
what he has , what he can
have , nothing that doesn't
clack . sometimes, pretending
vast wealth , I mull the
stuff over in my hands —
but mull is not the right
word. what can best give
one the idea — great wealth
and great poverty at the
same time . looking at what
he's got . looking at what's
got him , they are not
emphatically not one &
the same . what he has
is what I want , her —
what she has is what
she wants, , and I
don't have what I
want. i.e. I don't want
what I have.

jan 13.77

*

night clerk say
fantasies peak
at 3
is he the coach
for this
metaphysical stay ?

jan 14.77

*

I fail the impulses of civilization
it fails
it is stickiness
between the fingers
of a novel's pages

may be passed
back/forth
but not freed
from the literary

There is standing on my toes a bully
who is two bullies
they are one system
the system of make it
difficult for the bastard walk
meeting the force of his weight
their weights
I shunt them forward with me
that much resistance from my life
and the naturalness in me carries.

I shunt down the fall
for some obscure purpose.

jan 14/15.77

*

like the resistance offered by a suicide
during his trial last month I sat
smiled some of the time at Kathy
an equal amount at Anne
I wanted both equally; equally,
it was neither I wanted, only
any one of them . I wanted
the girl behind the lamp in
the next room . I wanted the
girl doing her trousseau by lamplight
high above the street in a
hotel room in another part of town
but You Kathy and You Anne
happened to be there so I wanted
you Kathy or You Anne . I am
not sure , perhaps if I'd been
somewhere else myself where
no-one was perhaps I would have
wanted no-one . If an easel had
been in a room with me I know
I would have advanced on it but
you cannot do that with two girls
each fights the other away from you.

jan 15.77

*

when the clocks begin to mambo
gold's bad algebra crystallizes
the system he uses to understand women.

Twice with a certain Susan was sadness
Once with two Susans in Boston
wasn't bad
but neither would have been enough
and both alone too much

and anyhow: 2 sadnesses
can be a joy.

I feel the hour.
like Hamlet: I feel the hour.

jan 16/17.77

*

ice being water , to which,
the water in which it is found
or the part of itself protruding into air
does the part of an iceberg
that is found
underwater, belong ?

jan 17/18.77

Photograph of Artie Gold by Christian Knudsen.

AFTERWORD

Artie Gold, one of Canada's finest poets, died on St. Valentine's Day, 2007. Gold, a member of the Vehicule Poets, died peacefully after a long battle with emphysema and most of the world.

Born in 1947 in Brockville, Ontario, Artie Gold, had been a presence on the Montreal poetry scene for over 30 years and even if he could not get around much in the last 10 years, his spirit still bicycled around the town he loved. He loved to roam the alleys in the middle of the night collecting the hidden value and beauty in other people's discard. He collected and displayed these, the world's knick-knacks, on his shelves, tables, in baggies and in his poems:

> I have knapsacks full of knick-knacks
> that spread beneath a tree
> would suffocate a hermit
>
> (untitled)

He prowled the night like his many cats; the cats he loved but who in return gave him not affection but allergies. He haunted all-night joints for that forever midnight connection, the conversations that went everywhere and forever. Many of us knew that when the phone rang too late for sleep it was Artie, the Gold, the Goldie, with an invitation to join him on these adventures or to listen to a quick poem he had just scribbled and had to share.

I've known Artie since the early '70s. And although we were in our mid-20s, he already had a reputation among poets as a "poet," the real thing. I first heard him read at The Karma Coffee House (like Artie, now gone). He amazed me with his wicked sense of phrasing, imagery and, later, when he showed me some of his already hundreds of poems, with his eccentric line breaks, frustrating spacing and punctuation. For these, and for everything else he wrote, he always had a perfectly golden reason.

Along with Ken Norris, we were the original poetry editors of Véhicule Press, although he considered himself the "disassociate" editor. He and I ran the Vehicule reading series in the early '70s. He was the disassociate host and when we started the mimeographed magazine *Mouse Eggs*, he contributed the name, some poems and his disassociation. And though he was always disassociating, he always believed in poetry as a noble obsession and in supporting the development of a vital and hip poetry scene.

Artie Gold wrote. And although he published only eight books, his published works were just the tip of the tip of the iceberg. Artie was always writing—on his manual Underwood, on the back of cigarette packs, on napkins, on the wall, on postcards to himself and to the rest of the world. He also sketched, sketches of the moment, the moment of a moment, like his poems, whose phrases and unsentimental melancholia left a permanent impression on your mind and in your heart. He and his poems made you realize that poetry, contrary to popular opinion, did matter.

Artie Gold was a poet who was sure of what he was. He paid rent in Fort Poetry. He, a wheezing asthmatic in the world, had such breadth in his poems that he could leave you breathless and wondering "how did he do that?" There was a Glenn Gould-Bach-like complexity mixed with a Rube Goldberg playfulness in his poems. His poems were city flowers growing between the cracks of this concrete island at the strangest and most arresting angles.

Artie did not conduct a particularly safe life. He took chances in life and in his art, which to him were one and the same. And though he wrote:

> I will hitch-hike out of here one day
> with my hair in my eyes and a good breeze blowing
> and cause a little confusion I'm sure-
>
> though no more than a hair
> discovered in a gravy.
>
> (untitled)

I disagree. Artie was more than a hair in the gravy, more like a pain in the heart. No picnic, Artie. Artie irritated life. He was engaged in the art of living with its urgencies and pleasures: on the turntable, Bach, on bookshelves, arranged by the architect of unsentimental sadness, the detectives of mysteries and the eccentrics of poetry. He was the city flower growing the way his few remaining strands of hair, always about to fly off. Artie, always a cat on a high wire fence, always with a poem, insisting to be let in but only on his terms, even if only to ransack your fridge and point to something beautiful, to something missing in your life.

Now, free of the allergies of this world, Artie, in the middle of winter, out on the balcony, a last cigarette, on the last train pulling out of town, on St. Valentine's Day, like a made up mind, is off.

— *Endre Farkas*

A Note on the Text

Those familiar with Artie Gold's poetry will not be surprised by his eccentric punctuation and spelling. Those encountering Gold's poetry for the first time may be baffled by what seems to be his erratic placing of periods, commas, semi-colons, colons, etc. Sometimes he places one of these markers immediately following the word, other times equidistant from two words, and still other times closer to the second word. This is partly due to his "Golden" rules of visual design on the page. His hyphens, em-dashes and two-dot ellipses follow similar rules.

In terms of spelling, Gold was neither a Canadian nor an American. He was a cross-border speller. This is a reflection of his literary and personal travels in Canada and the United States. The editors have decided to respect these "Golden" rules and leave the deciphering of his orthography and its significance to the critics and scholars who concern themselves with such eccentricities.

— The Editors

BOOKS BY ARTIE GOLD

cityflowers. delta can, 1974

Even yr photograph looks afraid of me. Talonbooks, 1975

Mixed Doubles (with Geoff Young). The Figures, 1976

5 Jockeypoems. The Word, 1977

some of the cat poems. CrossCountry Press, 1978

before Romantic Words. Véhicule Press, 1979

The Beautiful Chemical Waltz. The Muses' Company, 1992

The Hotel Victoria Poems. above/ground press, 2003